THE
STILL GOOD
HAND OF
GOD

Michael Gellert

THE STILL GOOD HAND OF GOD

THE MAGIC AND MYSTERY OF THE UNCONSCIOUS MIND

Nicolas-Hays, Inc.
York Beach, Maine

First published in 1991 by
Nicolas-Hays, Inc.
Box 612
York Beach, Maine 03910

Distributed to the trade by
Samuel Weiser, Inc.
Box 612
York Beach, Maine 03910

Library of Congress Cataloging-in-Publication Data

Gellert, Michael.
    The still good hand of God : the magic and mystery of
the unconscious mind / Michael Gellert.
        p.   cm.
    1. Psychology, Religious.   2. Experience (Reli-
gion)   3. Subconsciousness.   4. Psychoanalysis
and religion.   I. Title.
    BL53.G45 1991
    291.4′2′019--dc20   91-8024
                                                        CIP

ISBN 0-89254-020-6
MV

Cover art is entitled "Three Wishes,"
©1991 Ann Williams. Used by kind permission
of the artist.

Typeset in 11 pt. Palatino
Printed in the United States of America

CONTENTS

To my mother and father,

and

Arthur Webster

and

Denis Diniacopoulos

Funny how many claim to have the key to unlock the secrets of the universe—but where are those who will show, by example, where is the keyhole for their key?

—Osbert Moore

To get at the core of God at his greatest, one must first get into the core of himself at his least, for no one can know God who has not first known himself. Go to the depths of the soul, the secret place of the Most High, to the roots, to the heights; for all that God can do is focused there.

—Meister Eckhart

ACKNOWLEDGEMENTS

Many people have shared in the making of this book. Gary Granger, with whom I have enjoyed a spiritual comraderie for twenty years, contributed much time, critical reflection, and valuable insight, helping to elucidate some of the book's more difficult ideas. Also integral was George Gellert: he was always a source of encouragement, a wellspring of constructive suggestions, and a brother in the truest sense of the meaning. And Betty Lundsted, my publisher and editor, applied her wise discretion in details great and small, significantly influencing the book's discussion and helping to refine it into its present form.

I am particularly grateful to Susan Engel for introducing me to the Ann and Erlo van Waveren Foundation, and for providing other valuable assistance just when it was needed. To the Ann and Erlo van Waveren Foundation itself, I am most indebted. With its strong commitment to research in depth psychology and its generous fellowship, it was a source of both moral and financial support. And a word of deep appreciation goes to Dr. Aryeh Maidenbaum: he too was a steady source of encouragement and insight, and was helpful in more ways than he probably imagines.

Julie Mendlowitz, my loving companion through much of the book's creation, deserves heartfelt thanks for being very supportive and understanding about the demands placed upon my time. Alvin Muckley, Elizabeth Czerwinska, Susan Hochberg, and Lorraine Altman were also always ready to lend their listening ears and offer good cheer. For their very special ways of listening and dialoguing, I wish to acknowledge Nicole Corey, Dr. John Clark III, and Maggie Weintraub. And for contributing ideas that have enhanced the presentation of the text, I would like to thank Jerry Mendlowitz, David Deneau, Lucy Lentini, Natassia Cole, and Andy Sos.

There are other people who have touched my life in one way or another over the years, and though they did not contribute directly to the research or writing process, they helped me arrive at a place where I could sit down and write this book. They include Rabbi Izidor Lorincz, Dr. Paul Kugler, the late Koun Yamada-roshi, Barbara Sicherman, Dr. Paul Babarik, Brahm and Carole Canzer, Norman and Harriet Weinstein, and all my colleagues from District Council 37. The other friends and teachers who have helped in this way are too many to mention here, but I am sure they know who they are and how appreciative I am.

And finally, I wish to express my gratitude to some others who have provided material for this book. Lewis Freedman graciously made available his recorded interviews with Ingmar Bergman; Reynold Miller, Victor T., and Ellen S. shared personal experiences; the estate of General George Patton kindly gave me permission to quote from General Patton's poetry; and Random House let me use an excerpt from "Composition of Thus Spake Zarathustra" in Friedrich Nietzsche's *Ecce Homo and The Birth of Tragedy*, translated by Clifton P. Fadiman. Other authors to whom acknowledgements are due are: Donald Keene, for a quotation from his translation of the Japanese *Collection of Ten Thousand Leaves* (*Man'yōshū*); Raymond B. Blakney, for a passage from his *Meister Eckhart: A Modern Translation*, published by Harper & Row, 1941 (fragment 37, p. 246); and Osbert Moore, for an excerpt from *A Thinker's Notebook*.

FOREWORD

As a psychotherapist, I am often privileged to hear people's most intimate secrets. And often, I am impressed by how many of these secrets are of a religious nature. Surely, the very process of psychotherapy has a religious or spiritual character, for the courage to risk the changes demanded by psychotherapy raises issues which strike at the heart of our conception of life and the universe. Whether the world is perceived as friendly or antagonistic, and whether we can trust in some hidden "current" or force in life that helps things to work out positively, are issues which may be critical to the decision to risk change. Personal suffering such as trauma, illness, or the loss of a loved one also has a way of compelling us to examine our religious assumptions, particularly whether God exists and why he allows such suffering.[1] As a number of thinkers have shown, everybody has a personal religion or "mythology" insofar as they have a worldview that affects how they see the world and their place or destiny in it. How to find happiness or deal with suffering is as much a religious or spiritual question as a psychological one.

However, the emergence of religious or spiritual questions in the course of psychotherapy is very confusing for people, and, as I have observed, even for therapists them-

---

[1] I will refer to God in the traditional masculine gender for the sake of simplicity; no fixed image is intended.

selves. When these questions come on the tail of an experience which we would describe as "religious," matters become especially confusing. People do not know what such experiences mean—why and how they happened and what they imply about the nature of things—and therapists are often not equipped to help. This confusion may be compounded by the fear people sometimes have that such experiences are signs that they are losing their grip on reality. Because these experiences seem out-of-the-ordinary, people wonder if there may be something abnormal about having them.

The role of the therapist here must be to help people understand the distinction between losing their grip on reality and experiencing a different level or aspect of reality. I suspect that at least some of the current, fashionable "dumping" upon therapy and therapists occurs because the therapist doesn't address these concerns, and doesn't reach toward the kind of understanding of things that is needed in order to help people grow spiritually. But once these concerns and the confusion or fear around them are sufficiently addressed, religious experience can assume its rightful place in the process of psychotherapy. Its significance can be appreciated. This significance is manifold.

Perhaps the greatest value of religious experience is its intrinsic tendency to provide an additional perspective on life, including a change in perspective regarding the problems which originally brought us to therapy. It is not that life suddenly becomes better or paradisaic. Simply, things are seen in a larger or deeper context: they have meaning over and above themselves, or rather, they are seen as occurring in a world that has meaning over and above itself. The view that life and the world are the results of random events makes way for the view that the apparent randomness might have some order and purpose to it. It is this that ultimately helps, if not to end our suffering, to at least see it in a new light. Indeed, religious experience does not remove the pain of being human—of growing old, of watching creative energies peak and wane, of passing away and watching loved ones pass away. Rather, religious experience contrasts the human condition against the larger background of that which lasts forever. It helps us to see our condition for what it really is: a paradox. We are passing but lasting.

Another way in which religious experience can be most important for people is its capacity for self-empowerment. Unlike the religious dogma that holds that God is all-mighty and we are powerless and gravely limited, religious experience reveals that a real awareness of God's almightiness and majesty is indeed an experience, and as such occurs or flows from within. We experience ourselves as participants in God's radiance. In fact, we may even experience ourselves as epicenters of this radiance. I have more than once heard people who have had such illuminations jubilantly declare that they never imagined they could. To them, it has become evident that they are integrally connected to what is "over and above." They are connected not only by virtue of having had a religious experience, but in actual fact, in their psyches, in their *spirit*. This deepens their understanding of themselves, not in the usual, individualistic sense, but, as Heidegger would say, as "Being-in-the-world." This is self-empowerment but in a nonselfish way. And of course, this has an impact upon people's self-worth from a social point of view as well. All too often we are too eager to project upon others the capacity to have a religious experience, thinking that only "great souls" can have one: "Hermann Hesse can have one; Mahatma Gandhi can have one; Joan of Arc can have one; but I can't have one." It comes as a pleasant surprise to discover that "I can have one too."

The idea that religious experience occurs or flows from within forms the overall thrust of this book. Specifically, the central premise is that the unconscious mind is the seat of religious experience. Whether discovered through psychotherapy, artistic creativity, or any other endeavor or situation in life, the unconscious is that part of the mind that is inner-most within us.

This is as much a book about the unconscious as it is about religious experience. By approaching religious experience as a natural phenomenon of the mind as opposed to something foreign or supernatural, it becomes more acceptable and desirable. However, to establish religious experience as a natural phenomenon of the mind, we must redefine or broaden our concepts of both nature and the mind. St. Augustine said, "Miracles are not contrary to nature, they are only contrary to what we think we know about nature." Similarly, the experience of things ultimate and eternal is not contrary to the mind, but only to what we think is the mind. By broadening our understanding of what is natural, and in particular natural to the unconscious mind, we will be better able to appreciate religious experience as something that flows from within. It will become clear that religious experience is a realization of inner, hidden resources, and that it can deepen our self-knowledge precisely because it sheds light upon these deeper aspects of ourselves. Understanding the unconscious will furthermore help us to decipher what different kinds of religious experience mean—why and how they happen and what they imply about the universe and our place in it. All this speaks again to the idea of self-empowerment in its most spiritual sense.

A deeper understanding of ourselves and of the dynamics of religious experience is not the only fruit that can emerge from approaching the subject of religious experience from the viewpoint of the unconscious mind. We must assume that such an approach would foster speculation about the nature of God as well, for when we say the unconscious is the seat of religious experience, what does this imply about God? Does it mean that God is no longer the seat of religious experience, as has always been traditionally assumed? Does it mean that God doesn't exist, or at least remains unknowable, and that what we call "God" is really a projection of our unconscious minds? These are questions which cannot be evaded in an inquiry such as this. However, as centuries of such speculation have aptly demonstrated, there is no proof for the existence of God and no clear formulations on the nature of God other than our personal experiences. Although I hope to shed light on the above questions, my own subjective bias cannot be bypassed.

I have no intention of replacing God with the unconscious; rather, I wish to profile what may be the relation between God and the unconscious. A succinct way to describe this relation is to say that the unconscious is the matrix from which God reaches out to us. "Matrix" in Latin means "womb." God gives birth to himself—that is, enters into our lives—through our unconscious. This is both where the experience of him originates, or is "conceived," and where he resides until he is ready or we are ready for him to enter. It is my hope that this book will, by enhancing our openness and preparedness, contribute to our "readying" process.

A final word about my approach to the unconscious: to a large extent it will appear to be Jungian. Certainly, I draw a great deal from the insight of Jung, as he remains the foremost authority on the psychology of religion. However, as the reader will see, the approach I will take as the book progresses represents a radical departure from psychology as we know it, including Jung. The unconscious, I believe, is a far vaster phenomenon than even Jung imagined. In the final analysis, it should come as no surprise that the unconscious is a force as magical, mysterious, and ineffable as the supreme spirit to which it is, at its core, so intimately related.

Part I

FLOWERS OF PARADISE

*Tonight I am coming to visit you
in your dreams, and none will see
or question me—Be sure to
leave your door unlocked!*

—from the Japanese
*Collection of Ten Thousand Leaves
(Man'yōshū)*, ca. A.D. 750

INTRODUCTION

Since the beginning of recorded history, sleep has been looked upon as a deathlike occurrence during which we are suspended from the everyday world into another realm. Though the term "unconscious" may not have been used to describe this realm or state of suspension, the belief that our souls journeyed elsewhere during the night was universally prevalent. In the Bible, for example, dreams were seen as a medium for God, and those who were especially prone to having divinely inspired dreams were recognized as prophets, as voicepieces for God. More recently, the European Romantics, with whom the modern psychology of the unconscious had its origins, illustrated that our nocturnal minds are easier inclined to grasp, if not the divine itself, the rich assortment of images, ideas, and sentiments which clothe the divine. The unconscious imagination is, in the words of William Blake, "the world of eternity. It is the divine bosom into which we shall go after the death of the vegetated body."[1] Thus, to figures like Blake, the world of dreams was also really a "world" – a sphere or realm in its own right.

In light of this, I wonder if that other Romantic, Coleridge, was asking his question in anything less than a very

---

[1]Cited in Richard M. Bucke, Cosmic Consciousness, (New York: E.P. Dutton, 1969), p. 195. Also cited in W.M. Rossetti, *Prefatory Memoir of William Blake*.

real sense: "If a man could pass through Paradise in a dream, and have a flower presented to him as a pledge that his soul had really been there, and if he found that flower in his hand when he awoke—Ay! and what then?"[2] In dreaming the images and lyrics of his epic poem *Kubla Khan*, Coleridge certainly experienced the pleasure of awakening with a dream-flower in his hand. He gave testimony to the ancient as well as Romantic belief that when we sleep, our souls may cross the thresholds of other worlds and bring back with them things heretofore unimagined. Let us then contemplate Coleridge's question seriously: What if we actually awoke to some physical evidence that corroborated the workings of higher worlds, or other worlds, that were illumined in the dreams of the preceding night? Then we would be witness not only to the forces of creativity—as in the instance of dreaming a poem about Kubla Khan's life—but to the forces of the paranormal. What if, hypothetically, Coleridge's detailed dream of Kubla Khan was a dream of the *real* Kubla Khan? Is this possible? And ay, what then?

In Part I of this book we will entertain Coleridge's question in both its creative and paranormal prospects by devoting a chapter to each. The first chapter, however, will take a look at a strange hybrid of these two, wherein the flower is not exactly creative nor demonstrably paranormal, but something between the two and altogether different.

---

[2]Samuel Taylor Coleridge in E. Schneider, editor, *Samuel Taylor Coleridge: Selected Poetry and Prose* (Boulder, CO: Rinehart, 1951), p. 477.

CHAPTER 1

INTIMATIONS OF THE DIVINE

We have all had a magical experience at some time in our lives. It may have been a déjà vu, or a dream that came true, or an unusual coincidence—like thinking of somebody one hasn't heard from in years and then receiving a letter from that person the next day. Usually such incidents are dismissed as bizarre or purely accidental because they do not fit into the logical "scheme of things." Yet I think that many of us, when we have such an experience, secretly feel satisfaction and even a strange sense of familiarity, as if we have always known that such things were possible. These experiences are like "leaks" from another world, hinting to us the existence of a hidden order or truth beneath all that we take for granted as "reality."

Perhaps the chords of familiarity these experiences strike go back to childhood, a time when our conception of reality was not yet so well-formed and emptied of all that is magical. In my instance, I remember an experience from my childhood which is one of the most unusual I have had. It occurred when I was around 5 years old, and is one of my earliest memories. This is what I remember:

One night, in the middle of what seemed like deep sleep, I suddenly realized I was wide awake. I knew I was sleeping, but the sensation I had was not the sensation of dreaming, for I was keenly alert. I recall dwelling in this awareness for a few moments, until I sensed a presence

Figure 1. Sleep: a time when God — or one of his messengers — may come to visit. In the instance of St. Ursula, her vocation, martyrdom, and glorification (i.e., restoration in heaven) were announced to her in a dream. (Vittore Carpaccio, *The Dream of St. Ursula*, early 16th century, Venice, Accademia. Alinari/Art Resource, New York. Used by permission.)

which I immediately knew was God. I don't remember any particular qualities about this presence, other than that it was strong and seemed to be directly above and all around me.

Upon my recognizing his identity, God communicated to me. I remember this being on a nonverbal level—I just *knew* what he was "saying." First he confirmed his well-meaning intentions toward me—that he cared for me, that he would protect me and be with me my whole life. He then asked me if I would like to see what my life will be like, if I would like to see my future. I said yes. My entire life was then unveiled to me. I cannot totally recall how this was conveyed, but I do recall the passage of an extended span of time. I vaguely recollect a series of visual images of my future—like a speeded-up movie—flashing before my eyes. The meanings of the images were implicitly understood. But above all I believe what was conveyed was an overview of the "checkpoints" through which my life would pass, the landmarks that would give it its significance or character. And the basic message communicated was, "It's okay; it will be okay." I sensed God's guidance in the events of my life, that they would be occurring under his supervision or approval. I do recall the awareness of some anguish in the course of my life, but this too had God's mark of approval: it too was "okay" and was seen as just part of my life.

And then God "spoke." I believe he asked me if I was satisfied with what I saw. I said yes. And there was a shared sense of satisfaction, almost like a pact, an understanding between us. Then God said: "If you want to remember what you have seen, you must keep it a secret. You must tell no one." I said I understood, and the encounter ended. I do not remember if I then awoke or went into a period of ordinary sleep, though in the morning, when I got out of bed, the entire incident was vivid in my memory. I felt that something special had happened. I had been privileged with a special gift and I felt happy.

In the weeks that followed, a subtle change began to color my day-to-day awareness of events. I realized that what was revealed in my nocturnal experience was "true." Again, I do not remember exactly how I realized this. I believe that one or two events occurred which were forecast in the speeded-up movie, but because this movie was an overview of my entire life and only a few weeks had passed, and because I in fact do not remember the events, I imagine that they were not likely of major significance. In any case, I found myself having a curious sensation which I could not put into words until much later when, as an adult, I happened to read about the ancient Greek understanding of time. Very differently from ourselves, the Greeks, writes Robert Pirsig, "saw the future as something that came upon them from behind their backs, with the past receding away before their eyes."[1] As Pirsig adds, this may be more accurate than our modern metaphor in which we see ourselves facing the future, for the past is visible, the future is not.

In those weeks of my childhood, it was as if I were watching the already-existing future that was revealed behind me unfold into the past before me. It was like a déjà vu that did not end. Contrary to what one might expect, this did not rob my life of its spontaneity, but allowed me to really enjoy it. I was like a child who enjoys a story more and more with each new telling because I knew that no matter what happens, everything will turn out okay. Knowledge of the unknown gave me a kind of magical power to see that life was unfolding according to God's plan. I am aware that all this may appear to be a rather lofty percept for a 5-year-old mind. However, one should not underestimate how intelligent and sensitive—if inarticulate—children may be.

---

[1]Robert M. Pirsig, "An Author and Father Looks Ahead at the Past," *The New York Times Book Review*, New York, 1984. Also published in the 10th anniversary edition of Robert M. Pirsig, *Zen and the Art of Motorcycle Maintenance: An Inquiry into Values* (New York: Bantam Books, 1984).

When I treat children in my work as a psychotherapist I am often reminded of this. We have too quickly forgotten our childhoods, and with them the significance of Christ's adage that to little children "belongs the kingdom of God," and "whoever does not receive the kingdom of God like a child shall not enter it."[2]

Unfortunately, the kingdom of God did not last long for me. After a number of weeks, my cup had runneth over and I became cocky. It seemed to me that I had a firm grip on my discovery and could not lose it. With each day I became more convinced of the validity of my insight, and it became so integral to my awareness of things that it seemed inseparable from me. It was furthermore so "fantastic" that I could no longer keep it to myself. I had to tell somebody. My mother, who had taught me much of what I knew about God and religion and such matters, and who also happened to be one of my best friends, seemed like the choice candidate to whom I could entrust my secret. I thought that if ever I should need someone to recount its details—should I indeed be unable to remember them—she would be the ideal person to do so.

And so, the situation in which I chose to "test the Lord" and violate the condition upon which hinged my sacred knowledge was as follows. My mother was in the kitchen. It was afternoon. She was ironing clothes or preparing dinner or doing some other domestic activity. My baby brother was asleep in the bedroom, and so we were alone. I sat down at the kitchen table and announced to my mother that I had something to tell her. She acknowledged my request for her attention. I do not recall whether or not she stopped her activity; nevertheless, I remember being under the impression that she was listening with interest, as she had asked me some pertinent questions in the course of my relating my

---

[2]Mark 10: 14–15, Revised Standard Version.

experience to her. I told her of everything that had happened and that had been revealed to me. This is all I remember of this occasion.

❧

Now here emerges a critical time lapse in the reconstruction of my story. The following event occurred, but I cannot say how long after the above disclosure to my mother—it could have happened the next morning or it could have happened three weeks or three months later. All I know is that I woke up on a certain morning and I could not remember the details of my secret. I could remember everything except what God revealed to me about the future. At first I was terribly alarmed, but then took repose in the knowledge that my mother would surely be able to fill in the details. When I approached her, she could remember absolutely nothing about the discussion we had. She did not even recall having had it. I hounded her until I could finally accept that God's warning had in fact come true. To this day, all I remember is what I have written above. Of the revealed future, I remember nothing. As for my mother, when I periodically tell her this story, she listens with her usual, genuine interest, but only to conclude, "I'm sorry, I just don't remember."

❧

This story, like so many of its kind, can be easily explained as the product of a vivid imagination. There is nothing in it that proves the existence or activity of God. The fact that my mind was so integrally involved could lead to a variety of ways of interpreting this experience. If we are to be objective in attempting to understand it, we cannot rule out the more mundane, naturalistic explanations. Let's touch upon just a few.

To begin with, the entire experience reflects the emerging concerns of a 5-year-old child. At this age, a child begins to see that the world is no longer as idyllic and safe as he formerly thought. People grow old, people suffer from horrible diseases, people die. As Ernest Becker showed in his erudite study, *The Denial of Death*, anxiety over the body's vulnerability and mortality sets in at an early age.[3] There is much that is unknown "out there," as symbolized in the monsterish nightmares and "fear of darkness" so typical in early childhood. The developmental psychologist Jean Piaget tells us that the 5-year-old is in the "preoperational period" of cognitive development. During this time, dreams, fantasies, and intuitive, prelogical reasoning play a large part in the child's view of the world. The child may have imaginary companions, and invent stories and make-believe games that empower him and compensate against the harsh realities mentioned above. The child at this age is also beginning to move toward abstract thought, wrestling with such ideas as death, heaven, and God. As he integrates the concept of time, he increasingly talks about what he will become when he grows up, and the future becomes a real concern. In short, the 5-year-old has both the needs and abilities to produce a compensatory dream of a superparent God who reveals a future that confirms that everything will turn out all right.

Of course, if we espouse this view, there are certain peculiarities which we must also rationally explain. Firstly, I claim I was not dreaming, but consciously awake during sleep. How does one explain this? Very simply: I could have been *dreaming* that I was awake. Occasionally people recount dreams in which they dream they are dreaming, i.e., they dream of themselves asleep and having a dream. Usually this dream within a dream points to content of a very uncon-

---

[3]*The Denial of Death*, Ernest Becker, The Free Press (New York: Macmillan Publishing, Co., 1973).

scious, hidden nature, which is why the whole dream is presented like a multilayered onion. In my instance, it is not inconceivable that I dreamed the reverse, that I was awake—and we all know how real dreams can sometimes be. Or, also not inconceivable, I may have simply had an altered state of consciousness—a simulation of awakeness or a sort of visionary experience during sleep. Such possibilities also do not preclude the vivid imagination of the unconscious from participating.

Secondly, there is the question of a revealed future which later was experienced as "true" and then, in accord with the warning of the dream, mysteriously forgotten not only by me but an objective source, my mother. How does one explain all this? With regard to my mother, it is clear how she could forget. Perhaps she was more preoccupied with her domestic chore than I thought and was not really paying sufficient attention to remember. More likely, however, my story was, to her, one among many imaginative tales she regularly heard. I was, after all, a youngster living a large part of his life in the land of make-believe. How was she to know that this tale was no "ordinary" tale and not a fabrication? Probably she thought it was just another interesting story and forgot it with the others.

As for my own forgetting, it is difficult to fathom how this could occur with something that was previously so apparent to me. One possible explanation is that, somehow, there was implanted during the revelation state a post-hypnotic suggestion or implication that if I spoke I would forget. If my unconscious imparted such a message to my ego, it may have done so for reasons which C.G. Jung would describe as "archetypal." Jung's concept of the collective unconscious proposes that underneath a person's individual or personal unconscious (what Freud referred to as the unconscious repressed) there is an unconscious of the human race, an unconscious which all people inherit and which is more or less the same in everybody.[4] In this collective unconscious are stored many of the universal, religious ideas of history. Among these ideas or archetypes we would probably eventually find the motifs of initiation, the covenant, and betrayal. Initiation rites into the sacred mysteries of various traditions were usually shrouded in secrecy to safeguard the teachings from becoming commonplace or profane. A covenant or pact with the divine often had a heavy price, as observable in the ordeals of Abraham, Moses, and Christ, for example. And betrayal against the divine was always a possibility and, in the Old Testament at least, not without dire consequences. If we put these themes together, we may find ample material in the collective unconscious—yes, the collective unconscious of even a 5-year-old—to see from where might arise the idea of a taboo of secrecy which, if not honored, would lead to a violation of the pact and its benefits.

Can this be the background for the delayed mechanism of forgetting? Possibly. However, I must admit that this hypothesis of archetypal post-hypnotic suggestion is truly absurd, and there is no way I can substantially prove or shed further light upon it. On the other hand, perhaps only such an absurd solution would be fitting for such an absurd problem. As the early Church father Tertullian commented in regard to Christian theology, it "is to be believed because it is absurd."[5]

Still, if we are seeking a rational understanding, we are probably looking in the wrong direction. The problem of forgetting—in fact, the entire experience including the unusual perception of time—can be explained by one quick psychoanalytic stroke of the hand. In his early writings, Freud

---

[4]More will be said about these conceptions of the unconscious later; for now I am raising them merely for the purpose of our explanation.

[5]Cited in *Patrologiae Cursus Completus*, edited by Jacques Paul Migne, Latin Series, Paris, 1844–64, Vol. 2, column 751.

set forth his incest theory, which claimed that the symptoms of hysteria in certain cases may be traced back to childhood traumas of incest or sexual abuse. Later, Freud revised this theory—to the chagrin of many contemporary professionals who work with sexually abused children. In his revision, he asserted that the incidents need not have been historical. Instead, Freud now believed he was tracing the memories of *fantasies* of incest, and the cause of the pathology was unconscious guilt over these secretly desired fantasies on the part of the patient. In the same vein, perhaps what I am remembering is not an historical incident, but the *fantasy* of an incident. And in the world of fantasy, anything is possible.

Rationalistic explanations are important, for they keep things in perspective and curtail possible excesses in our desire to believe. Yet their danger lies in their tendency toward scientific reductionism, of reducing phenomena that may be very "large" into logical formulas that do not adequately capture the scope of the phenomena. The answers provided may be correct; it is the questions and their built-in assumptions that may be too narrowly framed. For example, if it is indeed true that in the world of fantasy anything is possible, might it not also be true that this would be an ideal world through which God could manifest and orchestrate the perception of events, if not the events themselves? Do events have to be real in order to be true? Perhaps God, too, likes to operate by one quick psychoanalytic stroke of the hand.

CHAPTER 2

THE GENIUS FACTOR

Throughout the ages, humankind has sought to identify the Mother of Invention, the source of creative discovery and innovation. Of course, today we know that there are many factors involved in the creative process, but most of us would agree that the factor that makes certain achievements glow with a brilliance unique unto them is the one called genius. But what is genius? Is it something we are born with—innate talent, a high IQ, a propensity to excel in a particular area? Certainly, it appears to include these things, for the great geniuses of history seem to have been blessed at birth with a rare capacity for excellence or an extraordinary imagination. However, this is a genetic view of genius, in and of itself devoid of the process of cultivation, a process which all of us can partake of and which can allow us to experience at least "streaks" of genius. What is this process?

I suspect that the process of cultivating genius is in large measure related to the unconscious. Many great scientists and artists acknowledge that it was not individual talent or sheer conscious effort alone that was responsible for their achievements, but also that subliminal "silent partner" to whom everybody has access. Thus, both levels of the mind were involved in the work of these scientists and artists, and though they may not have been at first aware of the hidden,

Figure 2. An illustration of the genius factor at work. Marc Chagall describes how the inspiration for this painting came to him one night after having fallen asleep:

> Suddenly, the ceiling opens and a winged creature descends with great commotion, filling the room with movement and clouds.
> A swish of wings fluttering.
> I think: an angel! I can't open my eyes; it's too bright, too luminous.

unconscious level, it soon enough became apparent that it was from here that their breakthrough insights came. One may think of scientists like the 19th-century chemist Friedrich Kekulé whose dream of a snake swallowing its tail led to the revolutionary discovery that certain molecules are not open structures but closed rings; or the 20th-century chemist Otto Loewi, whose dream of an experiment to demonstrate that nerve impulses are transmitted not only electrically but chemically won him the 1936 Nobel Prize in Physiology and Medicine.

In the visual arts, where dream imagery finds a most conducive medium, certain figures may also immediately come to mind. The names of Hieronymus Bosch, Marc Chagall, and Salvador Dali, for example, are synonymous with unconscious creativity. Yet even an artist like Edward Hopper, whose style is nowhere near as dreamlike and surrealistic, claims that, "So much of every art is an expression of the subconscious, that it seems to me most all of the important qualities are put there unconsciously, and little of importance by the conscious intellect."[1] And of course, there are people whose fields of endeavor are not scientific or artistic — or for that matter intellectual — but are nevertheless mentally demanding and creative. The professional golfer Jack Nick-

---

[1]Edward Hopper, letter to Charles H. Sawyer, Director of the Addison Gallery of American Art, 1939; in *Edward Hopper*, text by Lloyd Goodrich, (New York: Abradale Press/Harry N. Abrams, 1983), p. 152.

Figure 2. continued
> After rummaging about on all sides, he rises and passes through the opening in the ceiling, carrying with him all the light and the blue air.
> Once again it is dark. I wake up.
> My picture "The Apparition" evokes that dream.

The Apparition, 1917, oil on canvas, 157 × 140 cm. Ministry of Culture, Leningrad. Quotation from Marc Chagall, *My Life*, Orion Press, 1960, p. 82. (Originally published as *Ma Vie*, France, 1931.)

laus, for example, recaptured his winning profile after a streak of losses when he started swinging his golf club in a way he first saw himself doing in a dream: "I feel kind of foolish admitting it, but it really happened in a dream. All I had to do was change my grip just a little."[2]

In this chapter I would like to look at the genius factor of the unconscious, the magical ways by which it shows its wares, and how we may become sensitized to its workings, thereby cultivating it, inasmuch as this is possible, in our own lives.

✢

In 1893, a commotion developed in certain circles in response to an unusual archaeological discovery.[3] Many believed that psychic phenomena were involved. The University of Pennsylvania archaeologist Hermann V. Hilprecht, a specialist in Babylonian history, was putting the final touches on a book he was to publish that year. The book was about the findings of an excavation conducted by the University of Pennsylvania. A central discovery was the ruins of the ancient temple of Bel at Nippur (in modern-day Iraq). Hilprecht was attempting to decipher the writing on two small fragments of agate which were believed to belong to the finger rings of an ancient Babylonian. The fragments were found in the temple ruins, along with dozens of similar fragments. The cuneiform writing on these two fragments was missing many characters and lines. Further making matters difficult, Hilprecht was not working with the original remnants—which he had never seen—but from a rough sketch made by one of the members of the expedition. The most he could conclude from this limited information was

---

[2]"Happy Dream for Nicklaus: Jack's Back in Form," *San Francisco Chronicle*, Associated Press, Saturday, June 27, 1964, p. 37.
[3]All information and citations in regard to this discovery are taken from William Romaine Newbold, "Sub-Conscious Reasoning," *Proceedings of the Society for Psychical Research*, Vol. XII, 1896–97, London, pp. 13–18.

that the fragments were from the Cassite period of Babylonian history (ca. 1700–1140 B.C.), and that one of the fragments referred to the Babylonian King Kurigalzu. The other fragment which he could not decipher was presented in a section of his book reserved for unclassifiable fragments. However, Hilprecht was "far from satisfied" with this resolution, and wrote:

> The whole problem passed yet again through my mind that March evening before I placed my mark of approval under the last correction in the book. Even then I had come to no conclusion. About midnight, weary and exhausted, I went to bed and was soon in deep sleep. Then I dreamed the following remarkable dream. A tall thin priest of the old pre-christian Nippur, about forty years of age and clad in a simple abba, led me to the treasure chamber of the temple, on its south-east side. He went with me into a small, low-ceiled room without windows, in which there was a large wooden chest, while scraps of agate and lapis lazuli lay scattered on the floor. Here he addressed me as follows:—"The two fragments which you have published separately upon pages 22 and 26, belong together, are not finger rings, and their history is as follows. King Kurigalzu (ca. 1300 B.C.) once sent to the temple of Bel, among other articles of agate and lapis lazuli, an inscribed votive cylinder of agate. Then we priests suddenly received the command to make for the statue of the god Ninib a pair of earrings of agate. We were in great dismay, since there was no agate as raw material at hand. In order to execute the command there was nothing for us to do but cut the votive cylinder into three parts, thus making three rings, each of which contained a portion of the original inscription. The first two rings served as earrings for the statue of the god; the two fragments which have given you so much trouble are

portions of them. If you will put the two together you will have confirmation of my words. But the third ring you have not yet found in the course of your excavations and you will never find it." With this, the priest disappeared. I awoke at once and immediately told my wife the dream that I might not forget it.[4]

Hilprecht was uncertain what language the priest used in his discourse. He was confident that it was not the Babylonian language of Assyrian, and that it was either English or his native German. The next morning Hilprecht examined the fragments in light of his dream disclosures, and "to my astonishment found all the details of the dream precisely verified in so far as the means of verification were in my hands. The original inscription of the votive cylinder read: — 'To the god Ninib, son of Bel, his lord, had Kurigalzu, pontifex of Bel, presented this.' "[5] The missing, third ring which the priest said Hilprecht never would find had on it a portion of these words, but that portion was figured out by way of analogy to the many similar inscriptions found in the same excavation.

Hilprecht's discovery that the two fragments belonged together solved his problem. He was surprised not only by the unconscious origin of the solution, but by its rare likelihood, for, as Hilprecht explained, "There are not many of these votive cylinders. I had seen, all told, up to that evening, not more than two."[6]

Not entirely convinced of his discovery, Hilprecht, like any good scientist, had to see for himself if in fact the fragments fit together. Kekulé also once extolled such sound measures in a speech he delivered to the German Chemical Society. After describing his own dream discovery, he

---

[4]See Newbold's *Proceedings of the Society for Psychical Research*, pp. 14–15.
[5]From the *Proceedings of the Society for Psychical Research*, p. 15.
[6]From Newbold's *Proceedings of the Society for Psychical Research*, p. 15.

admonished his listeners: "Let us learn to dream, gentlemen; then perhaps we shall find the truth; but let us beware of publishing our dreams before they have been put to the proof by the waking understanding."[7] And so, Hilprecht relates:

> In August, 1893, I was sent by the Committee on the Babylonian Expedition to Constantinople (now Istanbul], to catalogue and study the objects got from Nippur and preserved there in the Imperial Museum. . . . Father Scheil, an Assyriologist from Paris, who had examined and arranged the articles excavated by us before me, had not recognised the fact that these fragments belonged together, and consequently I found one fragment in one case, and the other in a case far away from it. As soon as I found the fragments and put them together, the truth of the dream was demonstrated *ad oculos*—they had, in fact, once belonged to one and the same votive cylinder. As it had been originally of finely veined agate, the stonecutter's saw had accidentally divided the object in such a way that the whitish vein of the stone appeared only upon the one fragment and the larger grey surface upon the other. Thus I was able to explain Dr. Peters' discordant descriptions of the two fragments.[8]

Dr. Peters was a colleague of Hilprecht's. His "discordant descriptions" affirmed that the fragments were of different colors and hence in all likelihood from different objects.

One could imagine how this discovery led to the speculation that there had been supernatural forces at work here,

---

[7]Freidrich A. Kekulé, recorded in *Berichte, Deutsche Chemische Gesellschaft zu Berlin*, 1890, Vol. 23, p. 1306; translated into English by Francis R. Japp, "Kekulé Memorial Lecture," *Journal of the Chemical Society of London*, 1898, Vol. 73, p. 100.
[8]See *Proceedings of the Society for Psychical Research*, pp. 16–17.

that perhaps Hilprecht had indeed been "visited" by a priest from the Cassite period of Babylonian history. To correlate such disconnected facts and arrive at a cohesive and accurate conclusion may seem to be beyond the means of normal reasoning. But William Romaine Newbold, a colleague of Hilprecht's and an astute investigator of such matters, interviewed Hilprecht and with the latter's help unfathomed a more "worldly" explanation of how the discovery was made. To lay speculations to rest, Newbold published his findings in the *Proceedings of the Society for Psychical Research*.[9] He argued that none of the information obtained in the dream was "beyond the reach of the processes of associative reasoning which Professor Hilprecht daily employs," and that this information cannot be regarded "as ascertained by supernormal means." He also cited evidence that in 1891 Peters told Hilprecht about the discovery and location of a room "in which were remnants of a wooden box, while the floor was strewn with fragments of agate and lapis lazuli." Hilprecht later forgot this. (The psychologist Théodore Flournoy called the dreaming or cognition of information which appears new but in fact had been previously learned and forgotten "cryptomnesia." The "forgotten" information is thus stored in the unconscious.)

In conclusion, if the dream did not involve paranormal means of acquiring information, it did demonstrate the superb associative abilities of the unconscious: the unconscious induced various conclusions that the conscious mind did not; namely, that the rings were not finger rings but earrings, that they belonged together and were cut from a single cylinder—as rare as such cylinders are—and that the different colors of the fragments did not necessarily mean that the fragments were unrelated. These associative abilities are essentially of a mechanical or logical nature, yet they enabled the unconscious to literally piece together a puzzle

---

[9]William Romaine Newbold, *op. cit.*

buried by 3300 years of history. And needless to say, this was done in an appropriately magical and pleasing way—in the guise of a Babylonian priest in an ancient temple!

⁂

In the above-related incident, the unconscious accelerated the reasoning processes of the conscious mind to arrive at a discovery that the latter would probably also have arrived at were it given enough time. If Hilprecht would have had a computer to program all the pieces of information he had, it may very well have come up with the same conclusion. As remarkable as this computerlike quality of the unconscious may be, it is based on the interrelation of pieces or elements of information that already exist; it is not based on an original creation of something where before there was little or nothing. It is the latter kind of unconscious creativity that is most striking, for it shows not only intelligence on the part of the unconscious, but independent initiative and innovation. A curious example of this occurred while I was writing this book. From its inception, I had been struggling over what would be a good title for it. I had a few choices, but none seemed quite right. In the process of writing some of the material that appears later in the book, I was attempting to highlight the idea that God is still very much the active, benevolent force that the ancients proclaimed him to be. I wished to convey the impression that God can directly intervene in our affairs, that divine providence—God's guiding and tranquil presence in our lives—is real if we can see it.

One night in the course of this writing process, I had the following dream. I was sitting in the center of a theater; it was empty and silent, and there was nothing on the stage. Suddenly a man appeared from the left and pulled a large white movie screen across the stage. After this, he went to the side to get a ladder and a bucket of paint, and started to paint the following words in huge, red letters across the screen: "The Still Good Hand of God." Abruptly I awoke. Probing for a meaning to the dream, and particularly to the words on the screen, I realized they captured the theme I had been writing about at the time. The play on words was obvious. However, I also realized that they spoke to the overall theme of the book, that in a way, the unconscious was describing itself when it painted those words. And so, I had found a title, or rather, it had found me.

Many have experienced this kind of participation of the unconscious in the creative process. It can be quite magical, not to mention productive. The former Beatle, Paul McCartney, had this to say about how he composed his song *Yesterday*:

> It fell out of bed. I had a piano by my bedside and I . . . must have dreamed it, because I tumbled out of bed and put my hands on the piano keys and I had a tune in my head. It was just all there, a complete thing. I couldn't believe it. It came too easy. In fact, I didn't believe I'd written it. I thought maybe I'd heard it before, it was some other tune, and I went around for weeks playing the chords of the song for people, asking them, "Is this *like* something? I *think* I've written it." And people would say, "No, it's not like anything else, but it's good."
>
> I don't believe in magic as far as that kind of thing is concerned. I'm not into "Hey, what's you sign?" or any of that. But, I mean, magic as in "Where did you come from? How did you become the successful sperm out of 300,000,000?"—that's magic I believe in. I don't know how I got here, and I don't know how I write songs. I don't know why I breathe. God, magic, wonder. It just *is*. I love that kind of thought: All the information for a tree was in an acorn—the tree was somehow *in* there. . . .[10]

---

[10]Excerpted from the *Playboy* Interview: Paul & Linda McCartney, *Playboy* Magazine (December 1984), p. 107; copyright © 1984 by *Playboy*. All rights reserved. Reprinted with permission.

This is an interesting notion, that "All the information for a tree was in an acorn—the tree was somehow *in* there." Bob Dylan expresses the same with regard to his music. He feels that when he writes a song, "I got it some place. The song was there before I came along. I just sort of came and just sort of took it down with a pencil, but it was all there before I came around."[11] He believes a song "might have been there for thousands of years, sailing around in the mist, and one day I just tuned into it."[12] Of course, this sensation of "tuning into" an art form as opposed to creating it oneself is not restricted to musicians. J.R.R. Tolkien, referring to his magical fantasy tale, *The Lord of the Rings*, admits that, "I had very little particular, conscious, intellectual, intention in mind at any point. . . . I daresay something had been going on in the 'unconscious' for some time, and that accounts for my feeling throughout, especially when stuck, that I was not inventing but reporting (imperfectly) and had at times to wait till 'what really happened' came through."[13] The Nobel laureate Knut Hamsun, in his autobiographical novel, *Hunger*, also speaks of this sort of literary ingenuity. In particular, he describes an incident that was "like a vein opening, one word followed the other, arranged themselves in right order, created situations. . . . I wrote as if possessed, and filled one page after the other without a moment's pause. Thoughts poured in so abruptly. . . . and every word I set down came from somewhere else."[14]

---

[11]"Cited in Anthony Scaduto, *Dylan* (New York: New American Library, Signet Books, 1973), p. 141.

[12]"Bob Dylan," *The Rolling Stone Interviews, 1967–1980*, (New York: St. Martin's Press/Rolling Stone Press, Straight Arrow Publishers, Inc., 1981), p. 360.

[13]J.R.R. Tolkien, *Letters of J.R.R. Tolkien*, edited by Humphrey Carpenter with the assistance of Christopher Tolkien, (London: Unwin Hyman, 1981), pp. 211–12.

[14]Knut Hamsun, *Hunger*, (New York: Farrar, Straus & Giroux, 1967), p. 36.

One may wonder if the impressions of the above artists are not simply the airy ruminations that one would typically expect to flourish in contemporary popular culture. On the contrary, the antecedents of such thinking may be found in ancient Greece. The notion of the heavenly existence and pre-formed totality of a creative idea—be it a musical, literary, philosophical, or scientific idea—was entertained as early as Plato. Plato postulated the existence of a "supracelestial place"—a higher realm—in which are stored eternal "Ideas" or "Forms." It is upon these that the physical world of objects and the human world of perceptions, experiences, and creative ideas are modeled. Plato argued that by cultivating the mind through the discipline of philosophy, one may become sensitized to these Ideas and appreciate them as the matrix of creation and creativity.

Probably this Platonic view had its precursor in the earlier Homeric period in which the pantheon of gods and goddesses dominated the cosmology of the culture. During this time it was not uncommon for artists, poets, and philosophers to attribute their inspirations to an ethereal muse or daimon—essentially, a living guide in a nonhuman but nevertheless highly intelligent form. These homages were intended literally and not metaphorically. The mind was seen as fused with the spirit realm and subject to its workings. It is here that we may find the original meaning of the notion of genius. In Latin, the word *genius* refers to the guardian deity or spirit that watches over a person and influences him to produce great works. (*Genere*, from which *genius* is derived, means *to produce*.) The Romans, as the Greeks before them, believed that every person is assigned such a tutelary spirit at birth. By opening one's heart and mind to one's *genius*, one may receive the gifts of the latter's privileged knowledge.

In modern times, the residence of the genii has been relocated from outside and above to inside and below. The realm of the gods and Plato's supracelestial place are most

closely paralleled in Jung's concept of the collective unconscious; even the role of archetypes as models of human experience bears a resemblance to Plato's Ideas.

The collective unconscious, as mentioned in the previous chapter, underlies the personal unconscious, which in
turn underlies the ego. The ego is of course most accessible
to us, for it *is* us: the ego is the seat of everyday consciousness, of our emotional and intellectual functioning. It is also
the seat of our personalities, our individual identities. (In
Latin, *ego* means *I.*) The personal unconscious also belongs
to us, for it consists of all those thoughts, feelings, and experiences which we have forgotten or, on the other hand,
repressed because they were too painful or threatening to
our sense of well-being and self-image. This layer of the
unconscious is the cornerstone of Freud's psychology.

By contrast, the collective unconscious, the cornerstone
of Jung's psychology, is *not* us in the individualistic sense. It
does not come from conscious experience but precedes it. Its
information is ingrained into our psyches in much the same
way that other hereditary information is ingrained into our
genes. This information—the archetypes—is more or less
identical in everyone's unconscious. The archetypes mentioned earlier were the initiation, covenant, and betrayal
motifs. But there are hundreds of others. Jung in fact argues
that Freud's idea of the Oedipus complex is just such an
archetypal motif: "Oedipus gives you an excellent example
of the behavior of an archetype. It is always a whole situation. There is a mother; there is a father; there is a son; so
there is a whole story of how such a situation develops and
to what end it leads finally. That is an archetype."[15] Such
stories are the heritage of the entire human race. Their basic
formats are etched into the collective unconscious and

---

[15]C.G. Jung, in Richard I. Evans, *Conversations with Carl Jung*, (New York:
Van Nostrand, 1964), pp. 35–36.

passed down to us from generations and eons past. The collective unconscious thus serves as a rich storehouse of ancient information and knowledge.

This is one sense in which the collective unconscious is the realm of the genii. But there is another sense, one in which the archetypes actually function as genii. Jung provides an illustration of this in his memoirs when he describes his dream and fantasy encounters with *his* genius, Philemon:

> Philemon was a pagan and brought with him an Egypto-Hellenistic atmosphere with a Gnostic coloration. His figure first appeared to me in the following dream.
>
> There was a blue sky, like the sea, covered not by clouds but by flat brown clods of earth. It looked as if the clods were breaking apart and the blue water of the sea were becoming visible between them. But the water was the blue sky. Suddenly there appeared from the right a winged being sailing across the sky. I saw that it was an old man with the horns of a bull. He held a bunch of four keys, one of which he clutched as if he were about to open a lock. He had the wings of the kingfisher with its characteristic colors. . . .
>
> Philemon and other figures of my fantasies brought home to me the crucial insight that there are things in the psyche which I do not produce, but which produce themselves and have their own life. Philemon represented a force which was not myself. In my fantasies I held conversations with him, and he said things which I had not consciously thought. For I observed clearly that it was he who spoke, not I. . . . He confronted me in an objective manner, and I understood that there is something in me which can

say things that I do not know and do not intend, things which may even be directed against me.

Psychologically, Philemon represented superior insight. He was a mysterious figure to me. At times he seemed to me quite real, as if he were a living personality. I went walking up and down the garden with him, and to me he was what the Indians call a guru. . . . the fact was that he conveyed to me many an illuminating idea.[16]

One might easily be inclined to assume that the winged Philemon was an angel of some sort, or as Jung said, "a force which was not myself." In fact, when asked once in a film interview "What are archetypes?," Jung responded, half in jest but half seriously, "They are angels."[17] The serious part of his answer seemed to say that they are indeed forces that *appear* to us as angels. Certainly, their role is akin to angels if one considers the Greek origins of the word angel (*angelos*): it meant *messenger*. Archetypes are inner angels or messengers, and as Jung points out, though they are not produced by the ego, they do belong to the psyche-at-large, the unconscious. But what then are they? Where do they come from? In this, Jung's answer is as vague as the ancients': they just seem to be part of the structure and dynamics of the psyche. It is his characterization of them as *inner* phenomena that is novel, for with the advent of science we could no longer believe in a heaven up above, and thus such forces had to be stripped of their significance and denied. Demonstrating

---

[16]From *Memories, Dreams, Reflections* by C. G. Jung (pp. 182–84) recorded and edited by Aniela Jaffe, translated by Richard and Clara Winston. Translation copyright © 1961, 1962, 1963 by Random House, Inc. Reprinted by permission of Pantheon Books, a division of Random House, Inc.

[17]C. G. Jung, in Richard I. Evans, *Conversations with Carl Jung*. This part of the interview has been omitted in the book.

their psychological reality was one of Jung's central achievements.

Clearly, Jung perceived Philemon as a force emanating from and representing his own unconscious. Specifically, Philemon was a manifest form of what Jung called the self

Figure 3. Archetypes are inner angels or messengers. That angels were understood as inner phenomena even in the Middle Ages is suggested in this painting by Giotto. Here, Joachim, the father of the Virgin Mary, is having a dream in which an angel appears to him announcing that he will have a daughter. Although the angel is pictured externally, it is clear that Joachim is asleep and that this is an inner occurrence. (Giotto, *The Dream of Joachim*, early 14th century, Padua, Scrovegni Chapel. Alinari/Art Resource, New York. Used by permission.)

archetype, the higher, unconscious self that exists beyond the ego within all of us. In this sense, an archetype is very much like another personality within the psyche or a part of our own personality of which we are unaware. This idea of a plurality of personalities within the psyche goes back to one of the early pioneers of psychology, Sir Francis Galton, who observed how on certain occasions "dividuality replaces individuality, and one portion of the mind communicates with another portion as with a different person."[18] With Jung, however, this plurality became the main thrust of his psychology. He called these archetypal personalities "autonomous complexes," implying that they have an organized structure and energy of their own, and an independent life and will of their own. As a free agent apart from the ego, the archetype has a "quasi-consciousness" which, although not to be confused with ego-consciousness as we know it, effulges a distinct intelligence.[19]

These ideas, it may be said, introduced the equivalent of a Copernican revolution in psychology. Whereas formerly all unconscious phenomena were seen to revolve around the ego like the sun and planets were once believed to revolve around the earth, now it became apparent that the ego and archetypal complexes revolve around the self the way the earth and planets in fact do around the sun. This revision had two major effects. Firstly, it replaced the ego with the self as the center of the psychic "solar system," providing the ego with a higher mode of understanding towards which to aspire; and secondly, it relativized the perspective of the ego as one among many possible perspectives of how things may be looked at. These other perspectives do not diminish the

---

[18]Francis Galton, "Antechamber of Consciousness," reprinted in *Inquiries into Human Faculty*, (London: J.M. Dent and Sons Ltd., 1907), pp. 146–49.
[19]From *The Collected Works of C.G. Jung*, translated by R.F.C. Hull, Bollingen Series XX. Vol. 8, *The Structure and Dynamics of the Psyche*, pp. 190–92, 199. Copyright © 1960, 1969 by Princeton University Press.

ego but enrich it. These ideas also made a contribution to the study of religion and mythology by showing that the Olympian-like gods, goddesses, angels, and genii worshiped by most early civilizations—and in varying forms by primitive cultures—were really archetypal projections of the psyche. The pantheon of gods and goddesses was really the panoply of the diverse archetypes that populate our inner dream-world. As Joseph Campbell said, "Myths are public dreams; dreams are private myths."

⁂

The degree to which our inner genii really do "produce themselves" with a will of their own and say things that we have never thought is most curious. It is unsettling to discover we are not the sole inhabitants of our psyches, that "others" dwell there with us and often appear to have a more advanced intelligence. But what if we could indeed draw upon the knowledge and wisdom of these forces? What would such tutelage consist of, and what contribution could it make? For one thing, it might very likely have a strong influence upon our creativity—in particular, our religious creativity. In the following, I'd like to offer a few examples of this kind of tutelage and creativity. But before we proceed, it may be of value to briefly talk about some of the different modes of communication employed by the unconscious, since we will be reading about them. We have already referred to dreams and fantasies, though we have not actually discussed what they are. I would here also like to include a word about visions.

Dreams, fantasies, and visions are actually variations of the same "thing." They may be conceived on a continuum beginning with dreams, which occur in a sleep state and are hence the most common form of communication used by the unconscious. During sleep, the ego goes into a suspended state and submerges below the threshold of consciousness to allow the apprehension of unconscious contents. This apprehension is what we call a dream, though as Jung points out, "It is on the whole probable that we continually dream, but consciousness makes while waking such a noise that we do not hear it."[20] In other words, such unconscious activity is probably going on all the time; we merely do not perceive it when we are awake because the ego, now rejuvenated from sleep, has resurfaced and thrust us back into everyday consciousness and reality.

As the continuum moves toward the waking state, we find, less commonly, the occurrence of fantasies. They may occur in a hypnagogic (i.e., half-asleep, half-awake) state, or while we are completely awake but quite literally daydreaming. Some call this "free flow of consciousness," but for it to be a fantasy it must actually be an uncensored, free flow of *unconscious* contents *into* consciousness. The ego here does not submerge into the unconscious, but is relaxed and receptive enough to allow the latter to naturally surface. In this sense, a fantasy is not an illusion or whimsical fancy; it is an expression of the unconscious as genuine and valid as any other. The cultivation of fantasy, referred to by Jung as "active imagination," is a practice known for centuries among the world's great playwrights, story inventors, and novelists. We shall shortly see an example of this practice.

Visions are experiences of things which seem "out of this world" but which are literally *seen* to occur *in* the world. They often have an auditory component, and on occasion even an olfactory one. Visions are among the least common ways in which the unconscious manifests, and they occur clearly on the awake part of the continuum. In fact, Celia Green of the Institute of Psychophysical Research in England refers to

---

[20]C.G. Jung, *Kindertraumeseminar*, 1938–39, specially translated by R.F.C. Hull. Cited in Jolande Jacobi, *The Psychology of C. G. Jung*, (New Haven: Yale University Press, 1968), p. 73.

visions as "waking dreams."[21] Agreeing with her, the biologist Lyall Watson writes that almost all visions "occur as a result of dream-stream influences during consciousness, or of momentary aberrations in [the part of the brain which functions as] the synthesizer that coordinates and organizes normal conscious perception."[22] The term "aberration" is intended here in the biological sense, in the way that nature has natural aberrations or flaws. It is not intended in the sense of deviance. Though uncommon, visions are not a sign of mental deviance or pathology in and of themselves.

People, of course, hold varying views on what visions are. Some take them at face value for what they appear to be: objective apparitions or revelations happening "out there" in front of the viewer's eyes. Others offer an explanation more in line with the above. They are, like dreams, internal, psychological phenomena, but they occur in a conscious, awake state; they are thus *projected* externally—by the mind—to *appear* to be happening "out there," much like visual images projected onto a screen by a movie projector. The fact that people have claimed to have shared visions together is then explained as collective projections. In any event, however we choose to explain visions, we cannot deny that they are especially potent because they seem external and real.

Let us turn to the first of the aforementioned examples of creative tutelage by autonomous complexes. The writer Richard Bach offers an interesting account of how the ideas for his book *Jonathan Livingston Seagull* came to him. This book is about a seagull who leaves his flock to aspire to ever greater and greater heights of personal development (aptly symbolized through the metaphor of flight and the development of flying skills).

---

[21]Celia Green and C. McCreery, *Apparitions* (London: Hamish-Hamilton, 1975).
[22]Lyall Watson, *Lifetide: The Biology of the Unconscious* (New York: Simon & Schuster, 1979), p. 214.

One night in 1959, Bach was walking alone on a beach and heard a voice "behind and to the right" say: "Jonathan Livingston Seagull." Alarmed, Bach looked behind him but saw nobody. He went home and, sitting on his bed in contemplation of this strange occurrence, could only conclude that Jonathan Livingston was the name of a great racing pilot who lived in the 1930s. (Bach himself is an avid flyer.) Baffled, he said aloud: "Look, voice. If you think I know what this means, you're absolutely out of your mind. If it means something, tell me."[23] Immediately then, as Bach explains,

> I saw a very brilliant visual kind of dream while awake. I vividly saw a little seagull flying alone at sunrise, very much like the first major photograph in the book. I figured this obviously has got to be a Jonathan Livingston Seagull. And I didn't have to ask what his motivations were, why he's doing what he's doing. All in a split second I knew. It was like the great block of knowing we have in dreams sometimes—you just know. . . . It was like seeing a motion picture. . . . much of the dialogue I heard, too, including names.[24]

The vision that unfolded became the foundation of Bach's book. But the story he wrote at the time ended far short of its conclusion, and Bach comments that he "just couldn't think of a way to finish it."[25] Eight years passed with no further progress, and Bach had put the project aside. He did, however, write a freelance article on seagulls in which

---

[23]"It's a Bird! It's a Dream! It's Supergull!," *Time*, November 13, 1972, pp. 44–48 (Canadian issue). Copyright © 1972 Time, Inc. All rights reserved. Reprinted by permission from *Time*.

[24]Excerpted from an interview with Richard Bach that originally appeared in *Psychic* magazine, p. 6, September 1974, which became *New Realities* magazine in 1977. Copyright © 1974, New Realities, Limited Partnership. Used by permission.

[25]See *Time* magazine, November 13, 1972, p. 6.

he analyzed their flight skills. Then, one night in 1967, Bach had a vivid dream of seagulls. He awoke, and another vision occurred. He excitedly recorded it, and found that the new material fit together perfectly with the original material written eight years earlier. These together formed Part One of his book.

Parts Two and Three came later in a more ordinary way. Bach believes that the reason the book took eight years to complete was because the time was not ripe for such a book earlier—in regard to both his own development and society's receptivity to the ideals which the book promotes. In other words, he feels that the book was planned not only in its content but its timeliness.

What actually happened to Bach? Was the voice he heard another's, or was it the voice of an autonomous complex projected externally in much the same way a vision is? Bach answers this himself:

> I don't think it was an independent source such as an entity or guardian angel that some people talk about. I personally believe that in my instance it was part of the communication that goes on between units of my identity—aspects that exist at different levels.

> I believe there is one level of me—say that exists in a nonphysical dimension—that is very much aware and concerned with Richard Bach and knew that this idea of Jonathan existed and could be expressed. But it also knew that there was no way that Richard Bach of then was ever going to be able to accept the idea if it came to him in a normal way.[26]

---

[26]Excerpted from an interview with Richard Bach that originally appeared in *Psychic* magazine, pp. 8–9, September 1974, which became *New Realities* magazine in 1977. Copyright © 1974, New Realities, Limited Partnership. Used by permission.

In other words, Bach himself sees this experience as his own unconscious reaching out to him, divulging its superior insight in a way that would compel him to move toward and embrace it.

J.W. Dunne, the famous aeronautical designer and theoretician on the nature of time, provides an illuminating example of the kind of theological views the unconscious may advocate. In his autobiography, Dunne tells of a dream he had in which he was sitting on a hill overlooking the Jordan River.[27] On the other side of the river he could see a large number of people who represented humanity. The whole of that side was covered in shadow.

> The deep shadow was contrasted so strongly with the brilliant sunshine in which I sat, and ended so abruptly at the water's edge, that I became puzzled as to what might be the cause thereof. Then it dawned upon me that, about a hundred yards to my left and slightly behind me *God* was sitting working with bent head at something of which I was ignorant. I did not see Him because I could not turn my head: I merely knew that He was there. The whole scene was as silent as a picture. And the shadow which lay upon the world was the shadow of God.

> I must emphasize that I was, from first to last, fully aware that the vision was purely allegorical, and that all the images therein were merely conventional symbols. Had there been the slightest attempt to suggest to me that any of the figures were veridical— e.g. that God was a Male Worker—I should, probably, have shied away from the whole.

> I was deeply puzzled about one thing. *God's shadow was lying over the whole world. Then why did not those*

---

[27]J.W. Dunne, *Intrusions?* (London: Faber & Faber Ltd., 1955), pp. 121–24.

blind fools see it? As I asked myself this, I became aware, abruptly, that two yards to my left and just behind the limit of my field of sight, there was standing—an allegorical Angel. Do not ask me what he looked like; for that is quite unimportant. He symbolized something which could be questioned. And I fitted him with an allegorical make-up which would be in keeping with the rest of the vision. I made him a conventional Angel, tall, dark, beardless and attired in a long white garment. But I was not interested in him. Wild curiosity held me in its grip. I called to him and pointed. "Look! look!" I cried, "God's *shadow*! It's everywhere! It's all around them! Why, why don't they see it?"

I had expected that the reply would be something conventional about their being too much absorbed in their own, worldly affairs; and if that answer had come I should have discredited it; for my sympathies were with these people, and I knew that many of them were searching everywhere for evidence of God's existence. But the answer which came—came immediately in five, short decisive words—was completely unexpected.

"Because it has no edges," said the "Angel."

And I found myself wide awake—really awake—and memorizing carefully every detail of the dream. Of course, I saw at once that what the "Angel" had said was true. It is psychologically impossible to be aware of anything which "has no edges." To realize the existence of this or that there must be a "not-this" or "not-that" with which to make a comparison. As for the dream, it meant obviously that there was no place in the whole world where God is absent. Consequently, it would be useless to search anywhere for *evidence* of God.[28]

As Dunne himself indicates, the Angel and the portrait of God in his dream were facets of his mind. The Angel in particular, he emphasizes, "was so obviously a creature of my own imagination, constructed to accord with the supposed information he was conveying." Yet Dunne acknowledges that he "must give the 'Angel' his due: he . . . had shown me the possibility of there being a world-filling property of 'God.' "[29] An idea that had never occurred to him before, this became an important hypothesis – "the hypothesis of a single, space-filling Mind" – in his book *An Experiment with Time* (1927).[30]

For our final example we turn to the Swedish filmmaker Ingmar Bergman. In key respects, Bergman's experience marks a sharp contrast with Bach's and Dunne's. The following is from an interview Bergman gave to the American television producer Lewis Freedman. Bergman is here talking about how he conceived his film *Hour of the Wolf* (1967).

> BERGMAN: . . . I have always been interested in the function of our demons. I always have been interested in those voices inside you, and I think everybody has those voices and those forces. And I have

---

[28]Dunne, *Intrusions?*, pp. 121–123. Used by kind permission of Mrs. J.W. Dunne. Parts of Chapter XI have been omitted. Used by permission.

[29]*Intrusions?*, p. 123–24. Used by kind permission of Mrs. J. W. Dunne.

[30]Dunne had a number of further encounters with this Angel. In a dream not long before he died, he saw him in a scene that was pitch black with a raging tempest. Catching hold of the Angel's white robe, "I knew that it was the last time I should see him." Dunne then asked him a question which he had always been troubled by: "Christianity, is it true?" The Angel replied, "God lets it be true for those who want it to be true." Dunne had no concluding thoughts or comments on this response. See *Intrusions?*, pp. 143–44.

always wanted to put them in reality, to put them on the table.

FREEDMAN: Make them visible?

BERGMAN: Yes . . . exactly. And that's very strange—those demons—how they let themselves be created, how they have dimensions. They came very, very fast. Suddenly they were there, all of them, and I had difficulties in selecting them. They would come, all of them, about fifty, sixty.

FREEDMAN: That's amazing.

BERGMAN: And I wrote I think three or four books full of notes on people [demons in human form]. When I wrote them, I was sitting in a room; it was a very hot summer. The room was very quiet, silent, with shadows—I don't want to have the sun in the room when I write—and I slept there too; I had to finish. After two or three weeks I couldn't sleep there because *they were there*.

FREEDMAN: They wouldn't get out!?

BERGMAN: No, they wouldn't get out. They woke me in the night and they stood there in the "hour of the wolves," in the very early morning. And they talked to me. It was a very, very strange time. And then, after I made the picture, they absolutely went away.[31]

Obviously, Bergman had endured an intense immersion into his unconscious. The three or four notebooks he recorded during this period became the basis for his screenplay *Hour of the Wolf*. Through fantasies which actually

---

[31]"An Introduction to Ingmar Bergman," by Lewis Freedman, Executive Producer, Public Broadcast Laboratory Series, 1968. Used by permission.

became visions, Bergman was able to "conjure up"—actively imagine—his inner "people" or genii. Yet as creative as his experience may have been, most people would find it, to say the least, eerie. How do we explain the existence of *so many* people, and why were they, in this instance, "demons"?

Certainly, fifty or sixty is not a small number. Either the unconscious psyche is naturally very complex, or Bergman was suffering from multiple personality disorder—or both. To clarify this we may look to the psychologist James Hillman, who uses the term personification to signify the experiencing of one's subpersonalities. Hillman distinguishes between the personification of the psychopath with multiple personalities and the person who remains grounded in a strong ego but uses personification for purposes of growth. He explains the latter personification as "the paradox of admitting that all figures and feelings of the psyche are wholly 'mine,' while at the same time recognizing that these figures and feelings are free of my control and identity, not 'mine' at all."[32] Externalizing our inner "others" enables us to encounter them "out there"; in this way we can maintain a healthy distance and develop relationships with them (unlike the victim of multiple personality disorder who cannot maintain "ego boundaries" and *becomes* his personifications). Hillman stresses that the act of personifying must be thought of in its own right as a potential "way of knowing, especially knowing what is invisible, hidden in the heart. . . . Because personifying is an epistemology of the heart, a thought mode of feeling, we do wrong to judge it as inferior, archaic thinking appropriate only to those allowed emotive speech and affective logic—children, madmen, poets, and primitives."[33]

---

[32]James Hillman, *Re-Visioning Psychology* (New York: HarperCollins, 1975), p. 31.
[33]*Ibid.*, p. 15.

In other words, simply because deranged people experience personification does not mean that personification is, as we also discussed in connection to visions, evidence of derangement. Many things that disturbed people experience come from the unconscious *not* because the unconscious is the harbor for our disturbances (as is often one-sidedly believed), but because disturbances by nature churn up *all* kinds of things, conscious and unconscious alike. Madmen may indeed have bizarre dreams, yet when a poet has them, we condemn neither the dreams nor the poet. Thus, to answer our query about Bergman's state of mind, we may say that his experience points to the world of the poet *and* the madman, namely, to the innate complexes and complexity of the psyche. The difference between the artist and the madman is the *way* that world is beheld.[34]

As for the demonish quality of the complexes that manifested in Bergman's experience, we are compelled to

---

[34]There has been an inclination, particularly in the 1960's and 70's, to romanticize madness as a form of artistic or religious expression or as a twisted form of genius. The work of R.D. Laing is a case in hand. I do not support this tendency because I think it blurs the distinction between two very different ways of being. It is true that the line between art, mysticism, and genius, on the one hand, and madness, on the other, is sometimes very fine and that the states of mind they engender have certain similar features, but this line nevertheless needs to remain distinct. The person who has, as Bergman, immersed himself in the unconscious is a world apart from the person who has been altogether swallowed by it. A poetic way to contrast this difference is to say that the artist-mystic-genius possesses his madness, whereas the madman is possessed by it. However, "madness" is altogether probably the wrong word to use here. Most artist-mystic-genius types are not really crazy at all if one looks closely enough. They are simply, for lack of a better term, eccentric; but by "eccentric," I here intend the Greek, etymological meaning: "out of center." To me, this suggests "outside the center" of consciousness—social consciousness *and* ego-consciousness. Artists, mystics and geniuses seem to acquire their orientations from nontraditional and unconscious—or if you prefer, unknown—origins.

acknowledge the dark side of the human personality (what Jung called the shadow). As history has shown, our inner demons have as much a force and will of their own as our inner gods, as our positive aspirations. They include our fears and doubts, our hatred and propensity for violence of all kinds, our greed and envy, our selfishness and self-righteousness, our indifference and selective ignorance, and our laziness and avoidance of risking change—qualities which prevent us from attaining our higher potential and from helping others to attain theirs. Any newspaper can illustrate, in Hannah Arendt's words, "the banality of evil"—how widespread and commonplace these qualities are, how we have become inclined to take them for granted. And certainly within our own lives, we are, to varying degrees, unconscious of them.

As an artist, Bergman has striven to raise these qualities out of the unconscious and to allow them to speak. But why? Why cultivate these voices and even endow them with dimensions? Bergman gives a hint to the answer in his final remark, "after I made the picture, they absolutely went away." A similar thing occurred when he made *The Seventh Seal* (1956):

> When I had written the picture *The Seventh Seal*, I was terribly afraid of death. It scared me terribly. It was a madness. It was always behind my back as a shadow. Then I wrote *The Seventh Seal* without thinking of this fear. And after I had written this picture and made it, my fear of death had absolutely disappeared.[35]

In this film, Death was personified as a cunning, demonic angel with whom the hero of the story had to play a game of

---

[35]"An Introduction to Ingmar Bergman," by Lewis Freedman, Executive Producer, Public Broadcast Laboratory Series, 1968. Used by permission.

chess, the outcome of which would determine whether he would live or die depending on whether he won or lost.[36]

In both *The Seventh Seal* and *Hour of the Wolf*, Bergman's dialogue with his demons enabled him to integrate them into his consciousness—to face, understand, and accept them—in a therapeutically sound and wholesome way. By doing this, he transcended them; they disappeared. It is curious that especially after *Hour of the Wolf*, Bergman's films showed a noticeably increased concern with issues of love and human relationships, as if the humanizing of his demons somehow humanized Bergman himself. Indeed, these voices may tell us what needs to be understood and mastered, what needs to be healed, and this may pave the way toward loving. One may here think of Christ's words, "But I say unto you, That ye resist not evil."[37]

⚘

In the way of a conclusion, I should like to emphasize that we do not have to lock ourselves up in a room and deprive ourselves of sleep and sunlight in order to invoke the genius factor. In fact, sleep—that is, dreams—is not only the most common way through which the unconscious manifests, but also the most accessible. I am often asked by clients and students how they can become better sensitized to their dreams. Certainly, it appears as if the unconscious responds to our efforts to communicate with it as if it were another person. Even with those who do not easily remember their dreams, and even claim that they don't dream at all, the unconscious can be seen to spontaneously release dreams once this has been earnestly "requested." I do not believe that the unconscious can be manipulated to conform to our desires for it to produce dreams or a certain type of

---

[36]In the biblical tradition, not all angels are benevolent. Indeed, Satan is pictured as a "fallen angel."

[37]Matthew 5:39, King James Version.

dreams—e.g., creative, problem-solving dreams—for indeed, the unconscious seems to have its own autonomy. But I do believe what the mathematician Jules Henri Poincaré observed about the *interrelation* of conscious and unconscious activity.

Poincaré discovered the Fuchsian functions of mathematics based on a series of sudden intuitions which he felt arose from his unconscious. In his well-known essay "Mathematical Creation," he argued that if the conscious mind is intensely preoccupied with a problem or some area of activity, the unconscious will be inclined to pick up where the conscious mind leaves off and carry on the work of creative problem-solving.[38] (We saw this demonstrated in the experience of the archaeologist Hilprecht.) Along the same lines, to purposely "invite" our unconscious to participate in our conscious, creative activities *by making this invitation itself a conscious, creative activity* inclines the unconscious to participate that much more. The author Doris Lessing comments in regard to her own experience of this:

> I dream a great deal and I scrutinize my dreams. The more I scrutinize the more I dream. When I'm stuck in a book I deliberately dream. I knew a mathematician once who supplied his brain with information and worked it like a computer. I operate in a similar way. I fill my brain with the material for a new book, go to sleep, and I usually come up with a dream which resolves the dilemma. . . . The unconscious

---

[38]This essay was originally entitled "Mathematical Reasoning," and is found in Poincaré's book *Science and Method* (1908). George Bruce Halsted translated both the essay and the book from French into English. He called the book *The Foundations of Science* (Lancaster, PA: The Science Press, 1915).

artist who resides in our depths is a very economical individual.[39]

A method of dream invitation and scrutiny which I often recommend to clients and students involves keeping a dream journal. Although I am not generally enthusiastic about how-to methods (they tend to be simplistic and too quick-gratification oriented), I have found that the discipline and process of maintaining such a journal does help people better recall dreams. It also offers a way to engage the unconscious in problems we wish to work on—not only problems of creativity, but problems such as the kind Bergman was concerned with or the kind that affect our everyday lives, particularly our personal relationships.

Keeping a dream journal provides a context for introspection for people who wish to explore their dreams but are not in formal therapy or analysis. (It may also be helpful for people who are.) Often such introspection can lead to an understanding of problems from a different point of view, perhaps a point of view that is more balanced and objective and hence needed for the resolution of those problems. As Einstein is reported to have said, "The world that we have made as a result of the level of thinking we have done thus far creates problems that we cannot solve at the same level as

---

[39]Doris Lessing, *A Small Personal Voice: Essays, Reviews, Interviews,* edited by Paul Schlueter (New York: Alfred A. Knopf, 1975), pp. 66–67. Of course, Robert Louis Stevenson is also well-known for having cultivated a special, ongoing relationship with the "unconscious artist who resides in our depths." In a revealing autobiographical piece entitled "A Chapter on Dreams" (*Across the Plains,* 1910), Stevenson relates how he was "given" many of his stories—including *The Strange Case of Dr. Jekyll and Mr. Hyde*— by "the little people who manage man's internal theatre." He describes how he began "to dream in sequence and thus to lead a double life—one of the day, one of the night." This is to say that each night his dream stories commenced from where they ended the night before.

the level we created them at."[40] The unconscious may be a source to introduce a new and higher level of thinking.

Of course, many if not most dreams are difficult to understand because they are so densely disguised in abstruse symbols. Without question, symbols *are* the language of dreams, but unlike other languages this one has no fixed vocabulary to make easy translation possible (contrary to what some books on how to interpret dreams purport). One reason why dreams use symbolic language is because there may be *many* levels of thinking—many meanings—simultaneously present, and only a multilayered symbol can adequately encompass them. The ability to understand our dreams takes skill and time to develop, but is really not as unattainable as many think. In the exercises for keeping a dream journal, I include one of the more dynamic approaches currently used for making sense out of dreams. These exercises are presented in the Appendix.

---

[40]Cited in Ram Dass, *The Only Dance There Is* (Garden City, NY: Anchor Books, Doubleday, 1974), p. 38.

CHAPTER 3

UNTAPPED POSSIBILITIES

We are at a point in our understanding of the mind where we are beginning to acknowledge that it is capable of acting outside the scope of natural laws—at least *known* natural laws. Any event that occurs outside this scope is called paranormal, and precisely because it defies our understanding of the universe and its laws, our current scientific knowledge can be used only to roughly intimate how or why it, in fact, occurs. At best, our efforts to understand paranormal phenomena tend to be descriptive rather than clearly explanatory. We are still in the early stages of exploration, and it seems that what we know of the mind is barely the tip of the iceberg.

A number of important figures may come to mind when we think of the field of parapsychology: F. W. H. Myers, J. B. Rhine, J. W. Dunne, Paul Kammerer, C. G. Jung. Even Freud, who remained a skeptic most of his life, made a valuable contribution with his final acknowledgement of the existence of telepathy.[1] His theory that telepathy occurs as a function of the unconscious acting as a transmitter and

---

[1]Sigmund Freud, "Dreams and the Occult," *New Introductory Lectures on Psychoanalysis*, (London: Hogarth Press, 1934); originally published in Vienna, 1933. See also an interview Freud gave the Hungarian journalist Cornelius Tabori, published in Cornelius Tabori, *My Occult Diary* (London: Rider & Co., 1951), pp. 218–19.

receiver between two people—much like a telephone or radio—is still one of the strongholds in our thinking on this subject. In this chapter we will consider a theory of paranormal phenomena that is an amalgam of different theories from different fields. However, the focus will be less on theory than on the phenomena themselves and their exciting implications. As Sir Julian Huxley commented, "We must follow up all clues to the existence of untapped possibilities like extra-sensory perception. They may prove to be as important and extraordinary as the once unsuspected electrical possibilities of matter."[2] Our focus will thus be on how paranormal occurrences point to the untapped possibilities of the mind, revealing the mind to be far more than we ordinarily think.

🙊

When I was a college student, I participated in a workshop aimed at developing the latent resources of the mind. Psychologists tell us these resources make up 90 percent of our minds—the part which for our purposes may be conceived as the unconscious.[3] In the six sessions of the workshop, I was taught exercises to develop psychic abilities, particularly extrasensory perception, aura visualization, and out-of-body experiences (also known as astral projection). The exercises consisted of simple meditation and concentra-

---

[2]Sir Julian Huxley, "The Destiny of Man," *The Sunday Times*, London, September 7, 1958. Also cited in Rosalind Heywood, *The Infinite Hive: A Personal Record of Extra-Sensory Experiences* (London: Penguin Books Ltd., 1978), p. 107.

[3]Rollo May in this respect provides a rather comprehensive definition of the unconscious: "When I use the phrase 'the unconscious,' I, of course, mean it as a shorthand. There is no such thing as '*the* unconscious'; it is, rather, unconscious dimensions (or aspects or sources) of experience. I define this unconscious as *the potentialities for awareness or action which the individual cannot or will not actualize.*" (*The Courage to Create*, New York: W.W. Norton, 1975, p. 55.)

tion techniques, performed regularly for twenty to forty minutes once a day.

I will not go into detail about these techniques, not only because there is already an abundance of literature on them, but because I am, in retrospect, not so certain that they were in and of themselves responsible for the effects they supposedly produced. I believe that my special attentiveness to psychic phenomena may have been enough, for long after I stopped these exercises, such phenomena continued to occur with some regularity, as if to simply but genuinely acknowledge their potential invites them to manifest. In any case, the following series of events occurred beginning approximately four weeks after I started the meditation exercises. The workshop leaders informed us that we would most likely begin to observe manifestations of one particular psychic ability; which ability it would be would vary from individual to individual.

One evening, I was phoning a young lady whom I had met at a party to ask her for a date. I knew very little about her, except that she was attractive and seemed interesting. As the phone was ringing, *inside my mind* I "heard" her pick up the receiver and say "Hello." I heard myself say "Hello, Johanna? This is Michael Gellert. How are you?" To this she replied in a trembling, tearful voice, "I'm sorry. I can't speak to you now. My father just died." I heard myself say "I'm sorry. I'm really sorry. I'll call you another time." Now again, this conversation went on in my imagination while the phone was ringing. It must have rung seven or eight times. The imaginary conversation ended by the fifth or sixth ring. I thought to myself, "What a bizarre thing to think. Either I must be really nervous, or my mind must be twisted with wicked thoughts." The possibility of the latter gave me a shudder. However, I consoled myself that this was all absurd and dismissed the entire matter. At this point the ringing of the phone stopped. The voice on the other end said, "Hello." I said, "Hello, Johanna? This is Michael Gellert. How are you?" She replied, "I'm sorry. I can't speak to you now. My father just died." Her trembling, tearful voice was identical to the one I had heard in my imagination. The conversation concluded also the way I had heard it, and we said goodbye. Needless to say, I was shocked. To be told this kind of news was disturbing enough. To foresee it beforehand was even more disturbing.

As I later learned, Johanna's father died suddenly of a heart attack. He had no known history of a heart condition, and there was no way I could have intuited the fatal event through natural means. This was either a case of precognition or, possibly, telepathy.

Not long after this, another paranormal incident occurred. One afternoon I was getting into my car to visit a friend. As I reached for the handle of the door, a visual image suddenly arose in my mind and was superimposed upon the door of the car. In this image I saw the same door but it was severely smashed. I pulled my hand away in fear and the image vanished. I thought, "Is my mind trying to tell me something?" I had second thoughts about getting into the car, and drove especially carefully that day.

That evening, my friend and I went to a restaurant. I had parked on the street in front of the restaurant. When we came out, a crowd of people were huddled around the car; a police car was there. I made my way through the crowd and announced to the police officer that this was my car and asked if there was a problem. He said he was just passing by and happened to see a car—and he pointed to a car in front of mine with a man in it—sideswipe my car and continue without stopping, so he flagged the car down and made the driver back up to the "scene of the crime." It was at this point that I had come out. I looked at the damaged door of my car and was amazed to see that it identically matched the door in my "vision."

If I had smashed my door while I was driving, one could argue that this experience might have been a self-fulfilling prophecy. As it stands, I was nowhere near the scene of the accident, and my manner of parking was appropriately safe and such that it would not in and of itself cause an accident. I can only conclude that I had a precognitive experience.

The final incident in this series occurred a few days later. I was in a café one evening and was walking from one room to another. As I was passing the front door, I suddenly had the strongest feeling that if I would stop and turn toward the door, in a few seconds I would see an old friend whom I hadn't seen in years. Without resistance, I complied with my intuition. Sure enough, my friend walked in a few seconds later. When I told him what happened, he exclaimed that he had just been thinking of me.

⚘

Psychic phenomena like the kind described above may occur with more frequency than we recognize, for they may manifest in a way which escapes our conscious awareness. The writer Arthur Koestler took a special interest in such phenomena. In particular, he was intrigued by what he called "clustering" or "convergence effects"—coincidences of an unusual nature that occur in the environment but which seem to "echo" internal thoughts. Jung called this synchronicity. Koestler felt that in certain coincidences one would have to assume the existence not only of telepathic links between people but precognition. He cites some marvelous examples in his study, *The Challenge of Chance*. These, again, are of special interest for the manner in which they escaped the conscious awareness of the people involved:

> Mr. Adrian Bell is not only an eminent writer, but also the doyen of *The Times* team of ten crossword compilers. He spends about twelve hours on each puzzle and does one a week. Two days before the Soviet spy George Blake made his sensational escape from Wormwood Scrubs gaol [jail] by means of a car which was waiting for him in a narrow lane outside,

called Artillery Row, *The Times* published a cross-word composed by Adrian Bell. The solution of 4 *down* was "Gaol," and the solution of 27 *across* was "Artillery Row." Special Branch detectives interviewed Mr. Bell, but he had no clue as to what made him invent that clue.

The most remarkable cluster of coincidences—or echoes—appeared in the *Daily Telegraph*'s crossword columns immediately preceding the allied invasion of Europe—D-Day, June 6th, 1944. The codewords referring to various operations were perhaps the best kept secrets of the war. The codename for the entire invasion plan was *Overlord*. For the naval operations: *Neptune*. The two Normandy beaches chosen for landing the American task force were referred to as *Utah* and *Omaha*. And the artificial harbours that were to be placed in position off the beaches were called *Mulberry*.

The first codeword appeared in the solution of crossword 5775 in the *Daily Telegraph* of May 3rd: U T A H. The second on May 23rd: O M A H A. The third on May 31st: M U L B E R R Y. The fourth and fifth—the principal codewords—appeared *both* on June 2nd, four days before D-Day: N E P T U N E and O V E R L O R D.

MI5 [a branch of British intelligence] was called in to investigate. The crosswords had been composed by Mr. Leonard Sidney Dawe, a schoolmaster who lived in Leatherhead, Surrey. He had been the *Daily Telegraph*'s senior crossword compiler for more than twenty years. He had not known that the words he used were codewords, and he had not the foggiest idea how they had come into his head.[4]

Such occurrences may occur in dreams as well as in the public media. Katherine Taylor Craig writes: "That 'coming events' of national and even of international importance may and frequently do 'cast their shadows before' is a fact signalized by the dream-stuff that world happenings invariably furnish certain individuals."[5] Jung also noted how in the years prior to World War II an increasing number of his patients had violent dreams of a political, global nature. Possibly this had something to do with his coming to his senses and his re-examination of his initial inclination to view the Nazi uprising in an optimistic light—an error he later regretted and which many attributed to his political naiveté.

Undoubtedly many precognitive experiences occur before or during times of upheaval. They may come as forewarnings of life-threatening situations, if only we would take heed of them. Sir Winston Churchill on one occasion during World War II obeyed an intuitive impulse to sit opposite to the side where he usually sat in his chauffeur-driven car. A bomb fell near his car that night and were he sitting in his usual place he would most probably have been killed.[6] Abraham Lincoln, by contrast, had a different response to

---

[4]Alister Hardy, Robert Harvie and Arthur Koestler, *The Challenge of Chance: Experiments and Speculations* (London: Hutchinson Publishing Group, Ltd., 1973), pp. 200–201. Reprinted by permission of the Peters Fraser & Dunlop Group, Ltd.

[5]Katherine Taylor Craig, *The Fabric of Dreams: Dream Lore and Dream Interpretation, Ancient and Modern* (New York: E.P. Dutton, 1918), p. 119.

[6]Jack Fishman and W.H. Allen, *My Darling Clementine* (London: Pan Books, 1964), p. 136. Also cited in E. Douglas Dean, "Precognition and Retrocognition," in Edgar D. Mitchell, *Psychic Exploration: A Challenge for Science*, edited by John White (New York: G.P. Putnam's Sons, 1974), p. 169.

his precognitive experience. He recounted the following only a few days before his assassination:

About ten days ago, I retired very late. I had been up waiting for important dispatches from the front. I could not have been long in bed when I fell into a slumber, for I was weary. I soon began to dream. There seemed to be a death-like stillness about me. Then I heard subdued sobs, as if a number of people were weeping. I thought I left my bed and wandered downstairs. There the silence was broken by the same pitiful sobbing, but the mourners were invisible. I went from room to room; no living person was in sight, but the same mournful sounds of distress met me as I passed along. It was light in all the rooms; every object was familiar to me; but where were all the people who were grieving as if their hearts would break? I was puzzled and alarmed. What could be the meaning of all this? Determined to find the cause of a state of things so mysterious and so shocking, I kept on until I arrived at the East Room, which I entered. There I met with a sickening surprise. Before me was a catafalque, on which rested a corpse wrapped in funeral vestments. Around it were stationed soldiers who were acting as guards; and there was a throng of people, some gazing mournfully upon the corpse, whose face was covered, others weeping pitifully. "Who is dead in the White House?" I demanded of one of the soldiers. "The President," was his answer; "he was killed by an assassin!" Then came a loud burst of grief from the crowd, which awoke me from my dream. I slept no more that night; and although it was only a dream, I have been strangely annoyed by it ever since.[7]

Although Lincoln was annoyed by the dream, he denied its import and chose to interpret it as follows: "In this dream it was not me, but some other fellow, that was killed. It seems that this ghostly assassin tried his hand on some one else. . . . As long as this imaginary assassin continues to exercise himself on others *I* can stand it."[8] One might say Lincoln interpreted his dream too literally, which meant in fact that he did not interpret it literally enough, i.e., as pertaining to *him*.

Indeed, most dreams need to be carefully interpreted or, as explained in the Appendix, "amplified." But with prophetic dreams, rare as they may be, one should not be too cautious and critical. The difference could save one's life. Of course, when a dream seems to be symbolic in nature, it may appear simplistic to interpret it literally. But if no other interpretation feels right, one has to consider whether a literal one is perhaps appropriate. (In some instances, one may consider whether *more than one* interpretation is appropriate, for dreams can have multiple levels of meaning.)

A literal interpretation certainly was appropriate in the instance of the French film director Roger Vadim, who relates a dream in which he saw a friend being crushed to death in a train accident in a tunnel. This friend was soon scheduled to visit Vadim by train. Vadim told the dream to his wife Catherine Deneuve, who dismissed it as "simple Freudian symbolism." Vadim, however, could not see any symbolic significance in this instance. (As Freud himself said, "Sometimes a cigar is just a cigar," or to paraphrase, sometimes a tunnel is really a tunnel.) Vadim phoned his

---

[7]Ward Hill Lamon, *Recollections of Abraham Lincoln: 1847–1865*, edited by Dorothy Lamon (Chicago: A.C. McClurg and Co., 1895).
[8]*Ibid.*

friend, urging him to come by plane. The friend agreed. Vadim writes: "It was two hours after he landed that we heard about the derailment over the radio. The front car, in which he would have been sitting, was now just a pile of scrap iron. It was one of the most serious railway disasters of the time."[9]

꒰꒱

The enigma in all these experiences is the curious relationship between the unconscious and time. How can our unconscious divine the future? And is there in fact, as suggested by the childhood experience which I described in chapter 1, a future already formed and waiting to be divined? These are questions which strike at the very heart of our conception of reality. We believe ourselves to have free will, and such experiences point to a world whose events are predetermined and foreknowable. However, a closer look at the experiences of Churchill, Lincoln, and Vadim will reveal that we *do* have free will: all three men had choices, and had each selected different responses and exercised different precautionary attitudes, their choices might have had very different results. It therefore seems that in such cases—and we shall probe this issue again later from another angle—the unconscious is not divining events in which there is no room for free will to be exerted, but events precisely in which our free will is being called upon in order to make a significant difference.

Such seems to be the purpose of prophetic warnings from the unconscious. But as we have seen, not all prophetic manifestations of the unconscious are warnings. Certainly there were no warnings as such in my experiences, for there was little that could be done about the events that were forecasted. Like the occurrences cited by Koestler, they were

---

[9]Roger Vadim, *Bardot, Deneuve, Fonda: My Life with the Three Most Beautiful Women in the World* (New York: Simon & Schuster, 1986), pp. 185–86.

merely episodes of precognitive, extrasensory perception. Yet this still does not erase the problem about the future: does it or does it not exist in a preformed manner, and if it does, what is the relation of the unconscious to it? I would like to answer this question by offering another illustrative experience; it eloquently depicts the nature of time and the mind.

☙

Air Marshal Sir Victor Goddard was a man with impressive credentials. He studied at Cambridge University and the Imperial College of Science, London, and fought in World War I. His roles in connection with World War II varied: from 1938–39, Goddard served as the British Air Ministry's Deputy Director of Intelligence; from 1940–41, he was Director of Military Cooperation; from 1941–43, he was Chief of Air Staff in New Zealand and Commander of the Royal New Zealand Air Force; and from 1943–46, he was Air Officer in charge of Administration of the Air Command in Southeast Asia. Goddard was instrumental in fighting the Japanese in the South Pacific, India, and Burma. From 1946–48, Goddard was the Royal Air Force Representative at Washington, working with the Joint Chiefs of Staff. He retired from the military in 1951, pursuing a career in academics and writing. His books include *The Enigma of Menace* (1959), *Flight Towards Reality* (1975), and *Skies to Dunkirk: A Personal Memoir* (1982). In *Flight Towards Reality*, Goddard relates the following story:

> When I was flying south from Scotland, years ago, I came upon a disused airfield that suddenly became transformed and modernised—became its own, still-unplanned, future state—beneath my very eyes. I saw it there in finished form as fact.
>
> Please let me tell you of that happening.

I flew to Scotland, having planned to play golf at Gullane by the Forth. My aeroplane, a Hart, I left at Turnhouse, thirty miles away. Near Gullane was an airfield of World War I. Its name was Drem. Had it been usable I might have landed there instead. While in the neighbourhood, I motored there and saw the owner of the place and walked all round his farm—for that was what the airfield had reverted to. My purpose was to see if it would serve for a light aircraft when I came again.

I found the old airfield divided into many separate pastures by barbed wire, each being well populated with sheep or cattle, and one with pigs. The hangars were then nearing dereliction; they were all in use, as barns for hay and farm machinery, cow byres and chicken runs. It certainly no longer was a fit place for a landing or for housing any kind of aeroplane.

Next day—it was the very next, not more than sixteen hours later—my Hawker Hart and I approached, quite inadvertently, in hopefulness but in uncertainty, a gloomy silhouette of hangars in downpouring rain beneath black clouds which scarcely cleared the hangar roofs. I did not hope to land there; that never was my thought; I was intent upon no more than pin-pointing my position, for I had become disorientated while flying back to Andover and was many miles off course. The reason is irrelevant, but in spinning out of cloud about five minutes earlier I had nearly killed a girl wheeling a pram. She ducked to miss my scything wing-tip and I too seemed to be *uncomfortably near to death*.

Yes, this was Drem airfield, right enough—I recognised the hangars as I crossed the boundary fence at less than thirty feet in driving rain. Then suddenly the scene was lit with brilliant light which I supposed was sunshine. The airfield was clear, new-mown and clean, the nearest hangar doors were open and on the tarmac apron, wet from recent rain, stood, parked, four aeroplanes—three biplanes (Avro 504s) and then a monoplane of unknown type. Emerging through the hangar doors there was a second monoplane being pushed by two mechanics, one on the tail, one on the starboard wing. All five machines were brilliant yellow chrome. The mechanics who were there, attending them, were all in dungarees of blue.

I backed my "stick" to climb, to clear the hangar roof.

The year was 1935. We had no yellow aeroplanes in service then. Nor had we any monoplanes. Our airmen wore brown overalls. In all, I noted quite a dozen features of anomaly. The hangars had all been refurbished. The tarmac was all new. But what surprised me most of all in this surprising vision was the indifference of the airmen to my zooming over them at thirty feet. Not one of them looked up. But they were real men. The unreality to them must then have been myself and my quite-physical conveyance. No airman anywhere, on any tarmac in the world—that is, the world we think we know—could then have failed to look at me had I been *there* for him to see, and had my roaring Hawker Hart been *there* for him to hear. Those airmen did not pay the slightest heed to me or it.

I sped the length of that quadruple-hangar layout, traversing the roofs at speed. In seconds I had cleared the fourth and last of those four sets of "newly covered" buildings, then I was plunged again into the pouring rain; the vision had evaporated.[10]

Years later, in 1939, Goddard learned that Drem airfield had been rebuilt as part of the Royal Air Force's efforts to prepare for the war. The airfield was:

reopened as a flying training school with yellow Avro 504s and Magisters. The Magister was new; it was a trainer monoplane; it was the spitting image of the monoplanes I saw, that stormy day, four years before at Drem. None of that type existed back in 1935 – not in our normal consciousness. Meanwhile, our airmen's dungarees had also been transformed; no longer were they brown, but blue.

I realised, or recognised, this happening quite suddenly. It took me by surprise and shook me more alarmingly than had that vision shaken me when I experienced it in 1935. For I had then to rationalise the fact that time and happenings are not as I supposed. The training school at Drem and many features of its novelty were there as I had actually seen them several years before that school became a complex, active entity in space-time consciousness for everybody else.[11]

However, there was a discrepancy between Goddard's vision and the actual, rebuilt airfield. In questioning this, Goddard astutely gives us a clue as to what takes place in the mind during the precognition of future events:

---

[10]Victor Goddard, *Flight Towards Reality* (London: Thorsons Publishing Group, Turnstone Books, 1975), pp. 129–34. Italics are mine. Used by permission. Note that Goddard casually mentions his close call with death and sees its significance as "irrelevant." I am tempted to ask if his being "uncomfortably near to death" put him in a state of mind which somehow predisposed him to the experience which follows.
[11]*Ibid.*

The hangars which I saw in 1935 renewed and built in brick, as they were built originally, were actually, in 1938, rebuilt in steel. What can one say to that?—the plan that *was* to be accepted was that they should be left in brick? In fact, the brick ones were pulled down. The hangars that I saw in vision in that storm, were filling—would you say?—a thoughtform that was destined to be thought and then abandoned.[12]

If this is so, then Goddard's precognitive vision was not an apprehension of reality as it would be, but a *mental image*—a thoughtform—of reality as it *might* be (again diminishing the argument for absolute predeterminism). It was primarily the reality of the mind that was envisioned as opposed to reality itself, implying that this so-called future was as much a property of the mind as of the world. In fact, the real Drem may have been an equally available thoughtform—albeit the one that would be selected in the final run—and even had Goddard envisioned this one, it might still have been as much a property or phenomenon of the mind as of the world. This is no doubt a thorny concept and I will return to it shortly with elaborative viewpoints from psychology and physics. For the moment I would like to offer one more passage from Goddard which even further shows that the perception of the future is really a perception of *time*, time that exists *within the mind*, or if you prefer, exists as a dimension which the mind—the unconscious mind—can "sponge up" or siphon at random. Goddard writes:

Two English ladies, Miss Jourdain and her friend, Miss Moberly, were visiting Versailles and had a famous vision in the garden there.—Yes, both of them, I understand. Reportedly, they saw the place transformed to how it had been, near a century before. You know the story or have heard it, I expect.

---

[12]*Ibid.*

If so, you may have heard it was denounced as pho-
ney by someone who dug up evidence to show that
what the visionaries both claimed as having seen
was at some variance with the lay-out of the garden
at that time. But later there was found a plan for the
alteration of the garden which was dated prior to the
dating of the salient event which was enacted in the
vision seen. That plan was in conformity with what
the English ladies had described. That plan had been
prepared by the head gardener, but had not been
adopted at the time that he was sacked, and never
was. Presumably the gardener was still intent upon
his plan—his thoughtform—being realised. That
happening was a slip through time, but backwards.
Mine was a forward slip through time, at Drem.[13]

Goddard here speaks of the mind slipping through time. I
prefer, in order to avoid science fiction-type associations of
"time travel," to speak of this phenomenon in the way
described above. However, once we integrate the view of
time from modern physics, we will see that Goddard's
description and my own amount to the same. For now, the
significance of this passage is that the perception of the
future is no more extraordinary than the perception of the
past, given the hypothesis that both are aspects of time that
exists in the mind, or as a dimension accessible to the mind.

❧

Psychology and physics—the two fields I wish to draw
from in order to present a theory of precognitive
phenomena—represent very different worlds of experience.
Yet where the inner world and outer world meet is precisely
where these fields come face to face. However, before we
turn to their rendezvous, let us look at some of the more

13*Ibid*.

crucial ideas of each field. We begin again with Jung, for his belief that the unconscious is not an exclusively inner phenomenon is a good point from which to launch our inquiry.

We have already established that Jung conceived of the psyche as having three layers—the ego, the personal unconscious, and the collective unconscious. In fact, he conceived of it as having four. The fourth and deepest layer he called the "psychoid layer." It is actually the foundation layer of the collective unconscious. Jung believed that as the unconscious approaches this layer it is no longer purely psychic in nature, but "bottoms out" into the world: "The deeper 'layers' of the psyche lose their individual uniqueness as they retreat farther and farther into darkness. 'Lower down,' that is to say as they approach the autonomous functional systems, they become increasingly collective until they are universalized and extinguished in the body's materiality, i.e., in chemical substances. The body's carbon is simply carbon. Hence 'at bottom' the psyche is simply 'world.' "[14]

It is at and beyond this bottom level that the psychoid layer exists. In other words, where the psyche ends, the psychoid layer of the unconscious begins, meaning that in Jung's framework, the unconscious extends beyond the human psyche as we know it. This gives the unconscious an objective, ontological status in the world: it is "real." This is a radical idea, that the unconscious is greater than the psyche (which is why Jung referred to this layer as "psychoid," meaning "like the psyche" but not the psyche). Furthermore, Jung conceived of the psychoid layer not only as the "meeting place" of the psyche and the material world, but as the essential nature and common matrix of both. The psychoid

---

[14]From *The Collected Works of C.G. Jung,* translated by R.F.C. Hull, Bollingen Series XX. Vol. 9, I, *The Archetypes and the Collective Unconscious,* p. 173. Copyright © 1959, 1969 by Princeton University Press. Used by permission.

layer is basically Jung's answer to the ancient body-mind problem, which questions the relationship between matter and psyche, in particular, whether or not they are separate phenomena. Jung argues for the unity of these phenomena

Figure 4. The idea that the human being is fundamentally connected to the materiality of the world is suggested in this painting. Water is the source from which we both ontogenetically and phylogenetically emerged—ontogenetically, from the womb, and phylogenetically, from the waters in which all life on earth supposedly originated. Curiously, water is also an archetypal symbol for the unconscious. (Frantisek Kupka, *Water Lilies*, 1900. Musée National d'Art Moderne, Paris. Used by permission.)

by positing them as "two different aspects of one and the same thing"[15]—the psychoid layer.

In fact, Jung envisioned this layer of the unconscious as a transcendent, spiritual realm, an altogether third dimension at the core of the dimensions of matter and psyche. The psychoid layer actually pervades all of reality, and its topography or metaphorical location as a kind of "underground" entity should not be taken too literally. Of course, one might protest that Jung was here venturing into metaphysics, yet this concept allowed him to bridge the gap between the mind and physical, paranormal occurrences; for through the psychoid layer, an individual's mental processes may become extended not only into the material world, but to other individuals' minds which share the same psychoid layer. This might explain such paranormal phenomena as telepathy or synchronicity (for example, the fact that I thought of my friend in the café exactly at the same time he thought of me). However, this concept does not yet explain precognitive experiences like Goddard's; for this, we must turn to physics.

❧

To begin, modern physics points to a universe quite different from the one conveyed by our sense impressions. In this "new" universe, paranormal occurrences seem more plausible than in our traditional universe. The reason is because modern physics sees the two main building blocks of the universe—space and time—holistically and flexibly, whereas our senses and traditional logic allow us only a partial and fixed understanding.

In modern, Einsteinian physics, the three dimensions of space and the dimension of time are seen as a single dimen-

---

[15]From *The Collected Works of C.G. Jung,* translated by R.F.C. Hull, Bollingen Series XX. Vol. 8, *The Structure and Dynamics of the Psyche,* p. 215. Copyright © 1960, 1969 by Princeton University Press.

sion. Space and time are merged and inseparable. Space-time is envisioned as a field, meaning that the entire universe is a single entity, and all the objects in it (e.g., stars, planets, people, and the paper this is printed on) are variations in the field. The field is the universal ensemble of space, time, mass, motion, and energy. It is also the ensemble of all "sub-fields," e.g., gravitational fields and electromagnetic fields.

The unity of the field is most often conceived through the idea of energy. The field is the continuum of energy in the universe. Einstein and Leopold Infeld write:

> By far the greatest part of energy is concentrated in matter; but the field surrounding the particle also represents energy, though in an incomparably smaller quantity. We could therefore say: Matter is where the concentration of energy is great, field where the concentration of energy small. But if this is the case, then the difference between matter and field is a quantitative rather than a qualitative one. There is no sense in regarding matter and field as two qualities quite different from each other. We cannot imagine a definite surface separating distinctly field and matter. . . . What impresses our senses as matter is really a great concentration of energy into a comparatively small space. We could regard matter as the regions in space where the field is extremely strong.[16]

An illustration of how energy unifies the field is provided by the concept of waves.[17] It is known that all matter, when it vibrates, produces fluctuations in the gravitational

---

[16]Albert Einstein and Leopold Infeld, *The Evolution of Physics* (New York: Simon and Schuster, 1938), pp. 242–43.

[17]Theoretical illustration based on personal communications with Thomas A. Kovats, Montreal, 1976.

field called gravitational waves. Matter does this because it has mass. If the vibrating matter is electrically charged, it produces fluctuations or waves in the electromagnetic field. If the waves are fluctuating at one million cycles per second, they would be situated in the AM radio band. If they are fluctuating at a million-million cycles per second, there is an electric wave frequency referred to as infrared waves. If they are fluctuating at a hundred-million-million cycles per second, they are light waves. Radio waves, television waves, radar waves, light waves, x-ray waves, gamma waves, etc., are all the same "things": electric vibrations, ripples in the electromagnetic field that vary according to the frequency of the vibration charge in the field.[18]

The waves are "bends" in the field, like the bends or kinks on a warped, rippled coat hanger. However, there is a theory that matter itself may be made of extremely high frequency vibrations which have an appreciable amplitude or size in a very small region of space. In other words, matter may also be a kink in the field, a localization at a given point. A kink, in the context of matter, would be something in which the wave fluctuations are very rapid and sharp. Matter would be a dense, concentrated succession of these fluctuations. Figure 5 on page 70 depicts what would be the difference between light waves and "matter" or "particle waves." Thus, according to this theory, matter is part of the field; it may be described as space or field that is "all bundled

---

[18]The field is like a rope held between two people at a distance from each other, with one of them shaking it. The rope, or field, is rippling. Energy is transferred, but not matter. Waves are not really Point A to Point B "lines," as commonly illustrated in visual representations, but directional vibrations or movements of the whole field. The waves are pulses which travel through the field. The field is like a pond of water. If a rock is thrown in, energy pulses (waves) travel through the homogenous field (the pond), but no water is actually transferred.

up" (i.e., a kink). In this theory, matter and the universal field are unified. All is one.

The introduction of time into the field changes the latter's character significantly. The relativity theory demonstrates that time is fluid, that it changes according to velocity. For example, it is a fact that for pilots traveling at high speeds, time literally slows down. Although *they* do not experience it differently, sensitive atomic clocks aboard their jets indicate that time ticks slower for them while they are traveling than it does for the rest of us. The famous "twin paradox" of physics postulates that if one of two twins journeyed to a distant planet and back at a velocity approaching the speed of light, he would return much younger than his brother—even though the passage of time would have seemed the same to both of them.

It is perhaps with its overall view of time that physics makes its most bold statement. For physics claims that time, from the *universe's* point of view, so to speak, exists as a

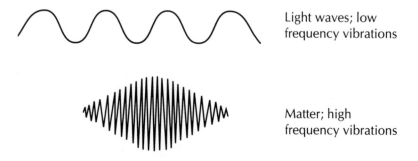

Light waves; low
frequency vibrations

Matter; high
frequency vibrations

Figure 5. The difference between light waves and particle waves. High frequency vibrations all "lumped" into a region have a property the slower, low frequency vibrations do not have: they "do" or "become something," namely, matter, mass. When a low frequency vibration, such as a light wave, hits a region where there is very high frequency, that is, matter, it is reflected. Similarly, water will not withstand high frequency vibrations, such as the matter of a canoe on its surface, without breaking up into particles.

single unit, an indivisible even if eternal instant. This is difficult for us to grasp because, as Einstein put it, "A human being is a part of the whole, called by us the 'Universe,' a part limited in time and space. He experiences himself, his thoughts and feelings as something separated from the rest—a kind of optical delusion of his consciousness."[19] The physicist Louis de Broglie adroitly explains this delusion: "In space-time, everything which for each of us constitutes the past, the present, and the future is given *en bloc*. . . . Each observer, as his time passes, discovers, so to speak, new slices of space-time which appear to him as successive aspects of the material world, though in reality the ensemble of events constituting space-time exist prior to his knowledge of them."[20] This *en bloc* conception of space-time is known as the Einstein-Minkowski or four-dimensional block universe.

We are here again confronted with the notion of the pre-existent formation of all temporal events, including future ones. An ideal metaphor to make this notion more tangible may be found in the principle of movies and books. A movie may last two hours; for our consciousness to cognitively process it, we must see it frame by frame. However, the fact of the matter is that this movie is contained *en bloc*, from beginning to end, on several reels of film. The movie can be picked up and carried in the hand. It is only our minds which must see it one frame at a time. Similarly, a novel consisting of 300 pages is "all there" in any given instant. Its reader may flip to page 299 and read the climax, but to understand how the story unfolds sequentially, the book must be read from the first page onwards.

---

[19]Albert Einstein, *New York Post*, November 28, 1972.
[20]Cited in P.A. Schilpp, ed., *Albert Einstein: Philosopher-Scientist* (Evanston, IL: The Library of Living Philosophers, 1949), p. 114.

Here we may bring together the ideas of psychology and physics in order to attempt an understanding of how precognitive phenomena may occur. Jung has already paved the way with his incisive suggestion that the space-time field is

Figure 6. This painting conveys the nature of time as an indivisible unit in the Einstein-Minkowski universe. Here, an entire day is presented in a single instant: all movements are simultaneously present; the sun can be located below the horizon in one place while the shadow cast by the knife suggests it is in another place; and the undulating motion of the waves can be seen even above the surface of the water, suggesting the changing tide of the ocean. Salvador Dali, *Nature Morte Vivante* (*Still Life, Fast Moving*), 1956. Oil on Canvas, 21 1/2 × 34 1/4". Used by permission of the Salvador Dali Museum, St. Petersburg, Florida USA.

actually a "psychically relative space-time continuum."[21] In other words, to Einstein's and Minkowski's mergence of space and time, Jung added the psyche. However, Jung's explanation of this is so terse as to be almost nonexistent, and he sheds no light on what might be the nature of such an interrelation between the psyche and the space-time field. Let's elucidate this idea.

We have seen that at the psychoid layer of the unconscious, the psyche "bottoms out" into the world-at-large; now if this world is a unified space-time field, and the psyche is connected to it, then we have a unified psyche-space-time field. And if time exists *en bloc* in the space-time field, then it also exists *en bloc* in the psyche-space-time field. This means that it is not inconceivable that at the psychoid level, which transcends what Einstein referred to as the optical delusion of consciousness, time may be represented in its totality—past, present, and future. It is possible that precognitive experiences are glimpses which the unconscious conveys to us from the deeper pools of the psyche- or psychoid-space-time field. These glimpses may very well consist of what Goddard called thoughtforms, for it is in fact not *the* future that is conveyed to us, but *images* of the future.

Figure 7 (on page 74) illustrates what a precognitive experience might be. Let us suppose that the box represents the block or a block of the psyche-space-time field. At a certain point, designated by the letter A, an individual is born. He goes through the winding course of his life's events until he leaves the psyche-space-time field as we know it, i.e., he dies. This occurs at point D. However, because time is all-contained as a single instant in this field, his unconscious may at a certain point in his life, designated as B,

---

[21]From *The Collected Works of C.G. Jung*, translated by R.F.C. Hull, Bollingen Series XX. Vol. 8, *The Structure and Dynamics of the Psyche*, p. 231. Copyright © 1960, 1969 Princeton University Press.

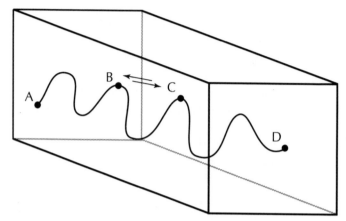

Figure 7. A block of the psyche-space-time field: a) is the point at which an individual is born; b) is the precognitive glimpse of a future incident; c) is the actual incident; and d) is the end of his life.

glimpse ahead to a future incident—or the thoughtform of a future incident—at point C; or reversely, the unconscious may project a glimpse of point C backward to him. In either case, this would be akin to opening the metaphorical book we spoke of to, let us say, page 250, and then returning to where we really are at in the story to catch up to page 250 in terms of our actual, day-to-day consciousness.

One way to conceive how this temporal travel of thoughtforms occurs—and I present this merely as food for thought—has to do with the preceding discussion on field-wave theory. Let us look at fig. 7 (the psyche-space-time field) in a different manner, one which sees the winding progression from point A to point D as a series of waves. Of course, this design is purely arbitrary and we are here adapting it to suit our purposes. This adaptation is not in the least overstretched when one considers, in the words of the physicist Thomas Kovats, that, "A wave is the name given to any process of communicating energy from one point to another without transporting matter from the first to the second point."[22] It seems that traveling thoughtforms fit this description.

Perhaps temporal thoughtforms travel as *waves* from the future or past. They would then in fact occur as facets of the entire psyche-space-time field *rippling*—or at least a block of it rippling. In the same fashion that radio waves or light waves travel through an oscillating electromagnetic field, perhaps thoughtforms travel through an oscillating psyche-space-time field. Perhaps science fiction would here have some proximity to fact, for this would resemble what has fictitiously been called a "time warp," except what we are describing above would actually be a "field warp."

It is curious that many precognitive experiences are, as indicated earlier, associated with an upcoming event of upheaval or trauma. Perhaps the approach of this causes a shock wave to ripple across the field from the future to the present, thus allowing the apprehension of a future thought-form. For example, if somebody were to have a car accident in four days, the shock of that *in four days* might, given the fact that it *already exists in the field*, generate a backlash effect to the present. This is assuming that the cause → effect stance of Newtonian physics is indeed no longer exclusively binding, and that an effect can occur prior to its cause and not only after (i.e., effect ← cause). If an effect is connected to a cause as a tail is to a dog—both existing in the field simultaneously—would not a door slamming on the tail cause the dog to bark? The principle of the future casting thoughtforms back to the present may also be illustrated by the image of a rock thrown into a pond sending waves back to the thrower. If an event in the pond or field is disturbing

---

[22]Thomas A. Kovats, "Models and Duality: The Eye and the Ear," in Denis Diniacopoulos, ed., *Arts and Science Monographs*, Vol. 1, Montreal, September 1976, p. 12.

enough, one might encounter the waves as he or she approaches the event. Both are already there.

All in all, these are theoretical speculations. Their value lies in making the bizarre a little less bizarre and perhaps more palatable to the logical faculty. An experience like God- dard's becomes more comprehensible with the understand- ing that the unconscious and time are unified. However, the existence of a psyche-space-time field can explain more than only precognitive experiences. For if the psychoid layer of the unconscious is an integral factor in this field, we must not overlook the possibility that the field is even greater in scope than heretofore imagined. Recalling Jung's conjecture that the psychoid layer is essentially a transcendent, spiritual realm, we may ourselves conjecture that if this is so, then the psychoid-space-time field is also unified with this transcen- dent, spiritual realm. In this way may certain paranormal occurrences exhibit qualities of a transcendent, spiritual order. Said otherwise, the theories we have speculated upon may lend weight to the notion that there are spiritual forces at work in certain paranormal experiences. Let us look at some of these experiences firsthand.

꒰꒱

Paranormal occurrences that suggest the intervention of a higher, spiritual order are very much like Rorschach tests: they mean different things to different people because they may be interpreted in a variety of ways. Without question, there is no paranormal occurrence that cannot by argument be attributed to purely psychological factors rather than to forces beyond the psyche. Especially in light of the theories set forth above, there exists a distinct possibility that the mind can be extended into the spatiotemporal realm, and thus it becomes increasingly difficult to separate what is mind and what is not. If the mind can project itself exter- nally, how do we draw a line between the internal and exter- nal, or rather, the intrapsychic and suprapsychic? Some closure upon this problem of what is within versus what is beyond should be gained as we proceed with the following chapters; for now, I raise it simply to acknowledge that it is the problem that above all others riddles our inquiries into the paranormal. Yet one thing is for certain about most paranormal events: they are generated by forces which are at least beyond the range of the ego or conscious mind. Even if such events reflect no more than the powers of the unconscious, they still reveal a great deal about the magnitude of these powers.

However, once we entertain the notion that certain paranormal phenomena display the involvement of higher, spiritual forces, we have to admit that our minds are indeed somehow connected or accessible to metaphysical levels of reality. This idea was conjectured early in psychology by Frederic W.H. Myers. (In religion and many traditions of philosophy the ultimate, metaphysical nature of the "soul" has of course long been assumed.) In 1891, Myers hypothesized that our consciousness is but a limited range within a much larger range or spectrum of possible consciousness.[23] Myers likened this spectrum to a thermometer and the normal range of consciousness to the short range of temperatures we humans know and live within on this planet: below our accustomed range, it is too cold, and above, too hot.

Jung later used the analogies of the ear's range of sound frequency and the eye's range of light perception to exemplify this idea of the lower and upper thresholds of consciousness.[24] Below the lower threshold is much of the physical world that we do not naturally perceive—molecules, cells, infrared waves, radioactive waves, etc. (though tech-

---

[23]Frederic W. H. Myers, "The Subliminal Consciousness," *Proceedings of the Society for Psychical Research, Vol. II, 1891–92*, London, pp. 306–307.
[24]From *The Collected Works of C.G. Jung*, translated by R.F.C. Hull, Bollingen Series XX. Vol. 8, *The Structure and Dynamics of the Psyche*, pp. 175 *ff*. Copyright © 1960, 1969 Princeton University Press.

nology has enabled us to venture somewhat into this region). Within the range of normal consciousness falls everything that constitutes our everyday awareness, as well as everything that could readily enter our awareness from the unconscious. This would include most paranormal phenomena. And finally, beyond the upper threshold of consciousness would extend the entire range of unknown, spiritual possibilities. It is above this threshold that paranormal phenomena of a spiritual nature would originate. Whether our minds momentarily rise above this threshold during the occurrence of such phenomena, or whether the latter descend into our consciousness from above, is of course unknown. I imagine that our relationship to higher levels of reality is a two-way street and that either case may be possible. Often, as we shall shortly see, these paranormal events seem to "come to us." Yet, as indicated by other kinds of experience such as altered states of consciousness, our minds can indeed expand and cross this threshold.

There exists a plethora of paranormal phenomena of a transcendent, spiritual nature. One of the more commonly experienced kinds is the supposed encounter with deceased human beings, i.e., the dead. One interesting account which clearly reveals the involvement of the unconscious is told by a colleague of mine, Reynold Miller. Miller is an ex-detective of the New York City Police Department and currently a psychiatric social worker in New York City. He shares his experience in the following:

> I am an African-American. My ancestors are from West Africa by way of the Caribbean (Barbados), and there are also Spanish-speaking members in my family. I grew up on the Upper East Side of New York City not only among North American black people, but Hispanics, Afro-Caribbeans, East Indians of Guyana, Trinidad and Jamaica (i.e., Asians), Italians, Irish and Jews. There were almost no majority-

culture persons in my world until late adolescence. The point I wish to make is that I come from a multi-cultural background in which the ethnic groups are by tradition closely connected to the spiritual side of life.

During the first quarter of 1986 I had an extremely trying situation concerning one of my children. It caused me great pain and concern. Quite contrary to the mores of my culture I kept quiet about it, feeling that the situation would best be resolved privately.

My youngest sister, who lives in Florida, had at this time a dream in which my deceased mother and one of my deceased sisters appeared, both with attitudes of grave concern. They said nothing. During the same period my mother, father and two sisters (all deceased) appeared in a dream to another sister who lives in the Bronx. Within the same time frame my father came to me in a dream, with a grave look on his countenance, a look of concern. However, he was calm and silent.

The dream of my sister in Florida caused her to wake up in the middle of the night. The next day she called my sister in the Bronx, and within a day's time they conducted a telephone poll of the other three siblings in New York. Of course, I confessed. Although I am the eldest, I was reprimanded for attempting to keep a secret regarding such a serious matter.

Events of this nature, i.e., prophetic dreams and warnings, are not outside the scope of our family experience. However, this was the first time that *all* deceased family members appeared in any of our dreams, and the first time these dreams occurred in *such a coordinated fashion* in response to a serious family problem. The value of these dreams lies in the fact

Figure 8. A visionary image of the afterlife. Perhaps the tunnel (commonly reported by people who have had near-death experiences) is representative of the unconscious—the phenomenon that connects us to the afterlife. Hieronymus Bosch, *Visions of the Hereafter: The Ascent into the Empyrean* (detail), 1500–1503. Palazzo Ducale, Venice.

that the gravity of the situation was communicated to all of us, but, in view of the calmness and silence, there was no suggestion of absolute despair, meaning here the death of my child. The dreams highlighted the need for concern, but essentially presented, at least to me, an outlook of hope and possible resolution.

I should like to add that many times during the danger-filled years when I worked as a policeman, I experienced warnings from significant deceased persons who were not family members. These warnings were conveyed not only through dreams but intuition and on one occasion an auditory manifestation (the voice of the deceased).

I find it difficult to accept the idea, so prevalent in the culture of this nation and our present times, that people cease to exist simply because they die. The idea of ancestors, family members and significant others having power to affect our lives is, to me, as natural as breathing. In fact, the feeling of connectedness between the living and those who have passed through the transition called "death" is an active part of the belief systems of many members of the African diaspora—as well as other peoples—all over the world. This connectedness makes me feel part of something larger than life as we know it. The older I become, the more convinced I am that this phenomenon is simply a part of my life experience, but a vital part which I prize highly. It celebrates the concept that life is everlasting.

Taken at face value, this experience suggests that the unconscious is accessible to what we call the "afterlife." This is to say that whatever spiritual realm the afterlife consists of, it too, in addition to the entire spatiotemporal realm of *this* life, is unified with the unconscious.

However, even if the afterlife makes itself available through such experiences, the subjective influence of the psyche still cannot be ruled out. For the psyche seems to perceive the afterlife in a manner that varies from individual to individual. Myers observed that when a deceased person is encountered simultaneously by a number of people, what is seen may be highly variable. In the following, Myers refers to the sighting of a deceased person as a phantasm:

> Our records of collective phantasms show at any rate that even when more persons than one perceive the phantasm it is not safe to conclude that *all* the persons present will perceive it. Nay, more; those who do perceive it will sometimes perceive it to different extents—one, for example, hearing only; another both hearing and seeing. It is even doubtful whether the perceptions of the different percipients are in all cases fully consistent with each other, or do not rather indicate that some initiating cause acts on each percipient in a manner determined by his own psychostatical condition. *Collectivity*, in short, is in such percipience more truly styled *electivity*.[25]

Sir Ernest Bennett provides a perfect illustration of this factor of inconsistency and electivity in his book on apparitions of the deceased. He tells of a landed lady who one day in 1926 visited a dying laborer from her estate. She attended with her steward and masseuse. After their visit they were passing along the shore of a lake when suddenly they saw, according to the lady, "an old man with a long white beard which floated in the wind, crossing to the other side of the lake. He appeared to be moving his arms, as though working a punt but there was no boat and he was just gliding along

---

[25]Frederic W. H. Myers, *op. cit.*, p. 320.

on the dark water."[26] All three saw him and unanimously agreed that he resembled the laborer they had just visited. Later they learned that the man died around the time of their vision.

Upon closer investigation of their accounts, certain discrepancies emerged. Contrary to what the lady saw, the steward saw the man not gliding across the water but walking. The masseuse witnessed "a shadowy, bent form step from the rushes, and into a boat." Assuming there was no dishonesty or error in perception on the part of the observers, they had clearly had separate experiences of the same event. Was this event the deceased soul actually appearing on the lake, or was it some other phenomenon *triggered* by the death or the dead person? Or was it simply the apprehensions of the lady, the steward, and the masseuse manifesting in an externalized way? Of course, there is no sure answer, but regardless of which explanation is the most likely, the unconscious mind undoubtedly played a strong role.[27]

---

[26]Ernest Bennett, *Apparitions and Haunted Houses* (London: Faber, 1939). This account is also cited in Lyall Watson, *op. cit.*, pp. 214–15.

[27]A relation between the afterlife and the unconscious is also suggested by the visions of former lives or incarnations which many people report. General George Patton, as one notable example, claimed he had numerous visions of himself as a soldier, *"In the form of many people/In all panoplies of time"* ("Through a Glass, Darkly," in Charles M. Province, *The Unknown Patton*, New York: Hippocrene Books, Inc., 1983, p. 247). Among his visions, he saw himself in a Greek infantry fighting against Cyrus the Great; in the Roman Legion; in medieval European battles; and in the role of a general serving under Napoleon's marshal Murat. However, as revealed in Goddard's account and as will be discussed in chapter 7, unconscious phenomena evincing historical or dramatic, true-storylike features may not always be what they appear to be, and thus, visions of past lives cannot be taken as *de facto* evidence for reincarnation or the continuity of life after death.

Figure 9. The marvel of orderedness in the cosmos, suggesting an underlying sentience as the ordering principle. Karl Friedrich Schinkel, *Queen of Night*.

Another kind of spiritual, paranormal experience which is very prevalent is the supposed encounter with what can best be described as the spiritual order within the cosmos. If not a contact with God himself, it is believed to be a contact with God's *design*. Though largely hidden, this design is conceived to be so orderly that there have evolved, in former centuries, complex systems of paranormal "logic" that attempt to mirror it and its orderedness. These systems include astrology, the Kabbalah of Jewish mysticism, the tarot (built upon astrology and the Kabbalah), palmistry, and the Chinese *I Ching* or *Book of Changes*. All are based on the premise that the spiritual principles influencing human events manifest also in other aspects of the universe, and if one can decipher some "map" to "decode" these principles via some physical parallel in the universe, then one has a paranormal key to understanding how human events unfold.

This parallel may be the constellation of the planets, the lines in one's hand, or the random way coins fall when we throw them in an uninhibited state of mind. The concept behind this is similar, for example, to the concept that underlies our thinking on the structure of DNA molecules in our cells. This structure exists not only in sperm and egg cells, but in all cells, thus making the idea of cloning a human being from a single skin or hair cell hypothetically possible. In systems of divination, the structure that is studied exists not only on the cellular or bodily level, but on the macrocosmic and spiritual levels; it pervades all levels. What is in the interrelation of the planets is also in the sphere of human affairs, or as the alchemical author Hermes Trismegistus asserted, "As above, so below." The connection between the human and cosmic levels is made by analogy of parallel occurrences. It is, as Jung writes, an acausal connection, which is why all these systems work on the principle of synchronicity or "meaningful coincidence."

Of course, in referring to divination, I am not speaking of the kind one encounters in the horoscope section of the newspaper. The Greek word *skopos*, at the root of "horoscope," means "watcher," and in traditional settings, a person who was a watcher was a serious observer. Systems of divination have today become vulgarized. The fact of the matter is that to truly master a system of divination such as astrology or the tarot requires considerable time and study. To cite an example, Nostradamus, the famous 16th-century astrologer, was a very learned man; to him, astrology was a "celestial science" as worthy of deliberation as the other disciplines in his repertoire, namely, Latin, Greek, Hebrew, mathematics, and medicine, the latter of which he had a degree in.[28]

To appreciate systems of divination in a serious or genuine way, one must take into consideration the foundation upon which they are constructed. Most people who see divination in a fortune-telling light believe it is founded upon predestination, but again, what is "predestination"? If an event is "registered" in the psyche-space-time field, does it mean that one has been absolutely preordained to live it out? An answer to this may be found in the Talmud. It states,

---

[28]Some of Nostradamus' predictions are uncanny: four hundred years before the birth of Hitler, he targeted a number of historic events having to do with the latter and even gave his name, spelling it as "Hister." So impressed was Goebbels — Hitler's Minister of Propaganda — with Nostradamus' writings that he commissioned an astrologer to extrapolate material from them to support Hitler's rise to power. (Evidently, the long-range implications of Nostradamus' prophecies eluded Goebbels and his Ministry, for Nostradamus also predicted the fall of Hitler.) However, in spite of their uncanniness, these predictions do remain subject to interpretation. The skeptic James Randi, for instance, argues that "Hister" was a Latin name for the Lower Danube River and that it is to this that Nostradamus was referring (*The Mask of Nostradamus*, New York: Charles Scribner's Sons, Macmillan Publishing Co., 1990, p. 213).

"Everything is foreseen, yet freedom of choice is granted."[29] It admonishes: "Do not think that because God knows what will happen things are predetermined and therefore a man is predestined to act as he does. It is not so. Man has the freedom to choose what he wants to do (Maimonides)."[30] Paradoxical as it may sound, foreknowledge is not predetermination. Simply, God knows what we will choose, but it is our choice.

For this reason, the Talmud also advises: "Pay no attention to the foolish and stupid things the astrologers tell you, to wit, the star in the ascendancy when a man is born, and the position of the planets at that time, determine whether he shall be wise or foolish, righteous or wicked, upright or crooked, strong or weak, rich or poor. . . . All these things are vanity and nonsense."[31] Yet I do not believe that it is with astrology per se that the Talmud is here opposed. The Kabbalah—which in regard to divination is based on the same principles as astrology—emerged alongside the tradition of the Talmud, and many Talmudists were Kabbalists. The opposition of the Talmud is rather with the *way* such systems are used: in turning to them to forecast the future, one tends to increasingly "buy into" the idea of a predetermined universe.[32] Living according to such an idea encourages a surrender of personal responsibility, an escape from freedom, as Erich Fromm would say. "It is meant to be," is what people who hold to this idea so often say.

---

[29]Cited in *The Living Talmud: The Wisdom of the Fathers and Its Classical Commentaries*, selected and translated with an essay by Judah Goldin (New York: New American Library, 1957), p. 141.

[30]*Ibid.*, p. 142.

[31]*Ibid.*, p. 110.

[32]Curiously, even Einstein, who was a key figure in promoting the idea of a predetermined universe in physics, had reservations about it: there is evidence that in his later years he questioned its applicability to human life and thus its universalism in general.

In using, or we could say abusing, systems of divination in this way, their most promising feature is undermined. A close look into most of these systems will reveal that their real foundation is not the force of predestination or a pre-established future, but the force of the unconscious or *the unknown in the present*. It is this that is actually being divined. It is this that is to a large extent the matrix of the future, the seed from which the fruits of the future are sown. Our possibilities—not just in terms of the future but in terms of human development—exist *in potentia* in the present, and it is to these possibilities that systems of divination speak. Approached in this way, oracles such as astrology, the tarot, and the *I Ching* are similar to dreams insofar as they are mediums for making the unconscious conscious. They do not dictate what will be, but rather illumine what could be by making us more aware of our choices and their possible consequences.

⚘

There are certain spiritual, paranormal encounters that resemble the above oracles in that they seem to be direct contacts with the design or "thought" of the cosmos and are experienced in an identical way—through the principle of synchronicity or purposeful coincidence. One such encounter is described in the following by a friend of mine, Gary Granger, a humanities professor at Vanier College in Montreal:

> In the summer of 1972, a very good friend of mine, a woman, had rented a chalet about sixty miles north of Montreal in the Laurentian Mountains, near a little town called Ste. Marguerite du Lac Masson. She invited me there several weekends and I eventually ended up spending most of the summer at that chalet. Being a teacher I had a lot of free time.
>
> One can only read so much, think so much, walk in the woods so much, and thus my mind started to

look for some kind of activity to pursue during the day. My friend would only come there on the weekends. Sometimes there were other people around on weekdays, but there were many long days with not much to do.

Years and years before, I had gone fishing a lot with my father and had quite a set of fishing equipment. It had been put away in a shed. Four or five times I had almost thrown it out. But I remembered it, and there was a little lake just behind the chalet. We had access to a rowboat. So basically what happened was that I started taking up fishing again. Sometimes I would get up in the morning and take a long walk, find a little stream or river in the vicinity, and fish. Some days I would just take the rowboat out on the lake.

After a few weeks, I started having moral reservations about doing this. It's hard to explain: it's messy. When I was 14 or 15, this didn't bother me at all. I didn't think in terms of how I was treating the fish or how the fish were suffering. It was just fishing; it was something men did. But at this stage of my life there was something about seeing the fish struggle, something about cutting into the body of the fish, getting blood all over my hands and directly causing death, that made me very uncomfortable.

This came to a head one evening around sunset after I had been fishing. I had caught three or four perch in the lake, and had left them on the stringer. The time came to clean them, that is, to cut off their heads, take off the scales and prepare them for cooking. Every time I had gotten to this point there was a kind of revulsion in me, but it seemed to me that this was part of the process of fishing—to clean the fish, that I myself had to do this, that it was part of what fishing involved. But I would put it off and put it off, and really all that did was cause the fish to suffer more. Eventually I would do it, but not very good-heartedly.

On this particular occasion, having done it, I really felt disgusted with the whole process, and it struck me that maybe I should give up fishing and find some other activity. I didn't know what it could be, but there had to be other things to do in the country besides killing small, defenseless creatures. I was really seeing the problem in this way. And I sat there outside the chalet, looking towards the lake, thinking: "Is it time for me to stop this? Enough is enough. I've seen what fishing is about and I really don't like it at this point in my life. Maybe when I was younger it was okay, but not now." I sat there and thought about this for a good half hour. I got very deep inside myself and eventually just said, "Give me a sign." I didn't know whom I was saying that to—to nature, to God; I just wanted some kind of a sign from outside myself to make it clear whether or not this was acceptable for me to do.

Having reached this point, I stood up and walked through the forest. There was a short path—maybe fifty or sixty feet—which led through the woods to the actual shore of the lake itself. I walked out on the dock, sat down, and said, "Now I want a sign." I started looking around the lake. It was quite beautiful. Sometimes there would be heron or bitterns. There was a beaver dam on the other shore and sometimes at sunset one could see the beavers swimming around, eating or whatever else they do. So I was looking around, and I looked up into the sky and saw something very unusual. There in the sky was a perfectly shaped fishhook. It was a cloud. It was isolated. There were some other clouds, far, far away to the left. But dead center in the sky, apparently hanging right over the lake, was a very large, long cloud perfectly shaped in the form of a fishhook. There was a barb, an eyelet, a long shank—to all intents and purposes, a fishhook—floating, above the lake.

As I looked at the cloud, I knew that it was my sign. And I also knew—I don't know *how* I knew, but I knew—that "it is okay." Fishing is okay as long as it is done in the proper spirit. It is part of the natural process to catch, clean, and consume the fish. The hook itself was ambiguous: there was nothing about the hook that implied an affirmative answer; there was no word "yes" written in the sky. The "yes" came from within me. But with the hook floating out there over the lake, I knew that Something or Somebody, somewhere, was aware of my dilemma and had responded to it. And the response—although again, I don't know how I knew this—was, "Yes, go ahead, it's okay."

Sometime later, I was reading an anthropology book which in one part discussed the hunting rituals of certain primitive peoples, such as Eskimos and African Pygmies. It was curious to discover how they saw all life forms as manifestations of the same spirit, and to kill an animal was like killing a relation of oneself. The hunter would thus say to the animal before killing it, "I am very sorry to do this, but I need your meat for food for my family. I send your spirit back to the Great Source, where you may continue to exist and from where you may return one day in another form." Reading this struck a peculiar chord with my own experience, and it occurred to me that there is such a thing as "killing with love."

The interesting thing about Granger's experience is that it is presented as a contact not only with God's design or will, but with God himself. Of course, as with any such experience, it can be explained as a mere coincidence or as the unconscious' ability to extend itself externally. Though from Granger's point of view, this incident was clearly *felt* to be a communication from the living intelligence of the cosmos. Reflecting on it, Granger believes it was an instance of "nature mysticism," which holds that nature (or the cosmos) has a mind and that this may be encountered directly. He believes his experience was triggered or "beckoned" by the intensity of his inner questioning, and that the "yes" answer was communicated intuitively through his unconscious.

If all this is so, this experience points to a unity between the human mind and the mind of the cosmos, or God. Such experiences of nature mysticism are not uncommon in the annals of history. One may think of figures like St. Francis of Assisi, Spinoza, Ralph Waldo Emerson, Walt Whitman, and Einstein. The example of Einstein is especially curious. In spite of the public's image of him as an athiest, he was obviously speaking for himself when he observed that "everyone who is seriously involved in the pursuit of science becomes convinced that a spirit is manifest in the laws of the Universe—a spirit vastly superior to that of man, and one in the face of which we with our modest powers must feel humble."[33] Thus, if pursued far enough, science itself reveals the heartbeat of a higher intelligence within the universe.

---

[33]Albert Einstein, *Albert Einstein: The Human Side*, edited by Helen Dukas and Banesh Hoffman (Princeton, NJ: Princeton University Press, 1979), p. 33.

Part II

MYSTERIUM TREMENDUM

*Provided one has the slightest remnant
of superstition left, one can hardly reject
completely the idea that one is the
mere incarnation, or mouthpiece, or medium
of some almighty power. The notion of revelation
describes the condition quite simply . . . .*

—Friedrich Nietzsche

INTRODUCTION

Mysterium tremendum, a Latin term made popular by the theologian Rudolf Otto, refers to the awesome mystery and power of God. To come face to face with this, Otto insists, gives us cause to tremble, for we are confronted by a force so profound that if it does not annihilate us, it annihilates our significance in light of it. It is this tremendous, numinous force that is at the center of religious experience. Ideas about God, belief in God, ritual observances dedicated to God, all are secondary to a direct experience of him. All may bring us closer to him, and thus may be of immense value, but none can substitute the palpable closeness of his Being as it brushes by us and makes its power felt in the depths of our souls.

However, it is apparent that the *mysterium tremendum* emanates not only from God, but from all that even remotely resembles God. One wonders if the *mysterium tremendum* is a quality only of God or if it is not also a quality of the unknown at large, gripping us in a spell of magnetic fascination. One may then even wonder if the *mysterium tremendum* is really a quality of "other" at all, if it is not really our own yearning acting upon us. Perhaps the *tremendum* is one of those mysterious things like beauty, existing in the eye of the beholder.

My own view is that the *mysterium tremendum* is a very real force. But when Yahweh said, "Thou shalt have no gods before me," he was inherently acknowledging the existence of other gods—and surely, in the Old Testament one comes upon numerous references to Baal, his chief competitor. Thus, it is possible that there is not only one *mysterium tremendum*, but many. It will be interesting to explore different kinds of *mysterium tremendum*, and to perhaps see what rationale, if any, lay behind Yahweh's jealousy.

CHAPTER 4

THE BELLY OF THE WHALE

In 1973, I took a trip through Asia. Like many Westerners who travel in the Third World, it was not my practice to carry a large sum of money on my person. Robbery is not uncommon, especially in the more impoverished countries, and even replacing stolen or lost traveler's checks can become a time-consuming and dubious affair. Thus, I traveled with no more than a thousand dollars on me—which at that time was usually more than adequate in these countries—and when I was running low, I would go to a Western bank in a big city and wire money from my bank in Canada.

On one occasion when I needed money, I had to go to Calcutta. It was not on my list of Most Desirable Places to See, but as I was coming up the Bay of Bengal coast from south India, it was the nearest big city with Western banks. I figured it would take about five days to get money.

It was April—pre-monsoon season. The rains were expected to begin in a few weeks, and by midday it would become unbearably hot and humid. The temperature would go over 100°F and the humidity would be in the 90–98 percent range. The sun would be towering overhead, and one could easily get a heatstroke or sunstroke if one were not careful.

Calcutta is one of the world's largest cities, with a population, in 1973, of over seven million. Under the British Empire, it became a prominent trading and commercial center, as well as the capital and major port of British India. In this century, the city has undergone great turmoil. Already overpopulated and ridden with pestilence and famine, the creation of East Pakistan in 1947 (now Bangladesh) led to an influx of millions of refugees, turning the city into an urban nightmare. Cyclones, floods, droughts, and earthquakes in the surrounding regions brought even more people. Conflict with China and war with Pakistan sent further waves of refugees.

Now, in 1973, poverty and despair continued to plague the city. Over five million people were crowded into insect- and rat-infested slums, many of which looked as if they had been bombed. Living conditions were appalling: buildings were decaying, walls and roofs were collapsing, and broken sewage pipes leaked through the asphalt-torn streets. Families were huddled into filthy tenements and huts with barely a few square feet per person. Running water and electricity were luxuries. Hundreds of thousands owned nothing but the shirts on their backs and camped in the streets, performing even their bathroom functions in public. Cholera and typhoid outbreaks were common—not to mention hepatitis, malaria, and rabies—as the city could not manage its sewage and refuse problems. Nutrition and medical care were of poor quality and in dire shortage. Many people had the appearance of walking skeletons, their legs so thin that one wondered how their bodies could be supported. I was shocked to see special trucks circulate the streets to pick up the bodies of the dead and abandoned, lying on the sidewalks as if they were a natural part of the landscape. But for the living, there was no easy exit: beggars, lepers, untouchables, and the severely disabled were in abundance. It would be years before Mother Teresa and others like her would have any impact on this situation; they were not even known yet.

To add to the above, I did not choose a particularly good time to visit. There had been strikes and riots during which it was dangerous to be on the streets. Apparently, there had been a number of deaths and the police were on alert. I did not know this until after I arrived.

In light of all this, I decided to settle my business as quickly as possible and move on in my travels. The city, of course, offered a variety of cultural activities to pursue—as it is, in spite of the poverty, one of India's great cultural centers—but given the physical, social, and political-economic climates, I did not feel especially inspired. I arrived on a Monday morning and went that afternoon to Barclays Bank. The bank official who was handling my request informed me that it would take three days for my money to arrive. This suited me fine; I thought I would take advantage of the opportunity and just rest. I was still recovering from a serious bout of dysentery during which I had lost almost twenty-five pounds.

Three days later, I returned to Barclays. The bank officer carefully explained to me the problem: Barclays wired my Canadian bank for my money. However, the intermediary agent through which the transaction had to go was not one which both banks mutually used. My bank used Irving Trust Company to send money abroad, and Barclays of India had no liaison with Irving Trust. (Barclays, a British bank, was operated, as all foreign banks, under Indian management.) My money had been wired to Irving Trust in New York, but from there could not be transferred to India. It was stuck in New York. The bank official explained to me that he had wired my bank with instructions to reroute the money through Manufacturers Hanover Trust, an agent which Barclays regularly used. The rerouting, including the upcoming weekend days, would take at least seven days, and possibly more. I was naturally annoyed at this development. I was also suspicious of the bank: I had heard stories that some Indian banks invested foreigners' monies on the international stock exchange for a few weeks – to earn profit – before they would actually hand over the money. And they would deceive the foreigners, the rightful owners, with all kinds of excuses.

Seven days would have been a long wait, so I decided to leave the city and return in a couple of weeks. I wanted to go to Darjeeling in the Himalayas. It would be cool there, and of course, the mountains are exquisite. As Darjeeling is in a special territory very close to the southern border of China, I would need a traveler's permit from the Indian government to go there. It took a day to receive this, and another day to stand in line and buy a train ticket to Darjeeling. I went to the bank, told the officer my plans, and stated in an emphatic but polite way that I expected my money to be waiting for me when I returned.

᪂

My train to Darjeeling was leaving on a Monday evening. I had planned to walk to the station from the hotel where I was staying – a half hour walk at a brisk pace – but on the way my leather sandal tore and I could no longer walk in it. I was unaccustomed to walking the streets barefoot, and so I tried to hail a taxi or rickshaw. However, rush hour had arrived.

The city was like a hive of mad bees. The profusion of traffic droned the senses: cars, taxis, streetcars and double-decker buses with people hanging out of the sides and windows, trucks, horse carriages, oxcarts, handcarts, tricycle rickshaws, manpowered rickshaws, motorcycles, bicycles, buffalos, cows, and last but certainly not least, an endless mass of people. The sound of horns honking, bicycles clanking into one another, and pedestrians and vehicle drivers shouting at one another made my head throb. And the air was staggering: it was so hot and thick with humidity that it was hard to breathe. I was drenched in perspiration.

It took fifteen minutes to find an available rickshaw, and with the congestion of traffic, another twenty minutes to get to the station. Clearly, I had not planned my departure well. As I ran to the railway platform, I could see my train two hundred yards away, accelerating with speed. I had missed it. I stood there cursing with anger and frustration.

There would not be another train until the next day, but first I would have to stand in line again for six or seven hours to get a new ticket. I did not relish this prospect, and decided to try my luck and go to the bus depot to see if there was a bus leaving soon for Ranaghat—the first train stop about an hour north of Calcutta. I knew that the train I had just missed would be stopping for a short while at Ranaghat, and I thought maybe I could catch it there. If I missed the connection, I could board the next train at Ranaghat.

At the Calcutta train station, it was so crowded that I could only get a rickshaw if I shared it with a few people. The driver would let me off first at the bus depot. Now at this point I could only guess what happened. I was in an extremely agitated state, which I suppose distracted me.

I was traveling with a small shoulder bag that contained my personal belongings—clothes, a sheet and blanket to sleep in, bathroom items, and a couple of books. I preferred to travel light; I did not even have a camera at this point. Now I had for much of the six months I was traveling kept my money, passport, health certificate, and other travel documents—the essential valuables—in a money belt that fitted around my waist underneath my pants. However, I had found this to be rather hot and clumsy in the pre-monsoon heat of India, and so now I carried these valuables in a small leather pouch which hung from my neck on my side. (This was separate from my shoulder bag and in cooler weather I would wear it underneath my shirt.) It is possible that in the crowded rickshaw it slipped off. Or the strap may have torn. Or, not unlikely, the following scenario: one of the fellows I was sitting with had deliberately sought me out at the train station, taken the rickshaw with me, and deftly cut the strap with a razor and taken the pouch without my noticing. (This fine art is known to provide many with their livelihood.) In any event, I only realized the pouch was gone when I was at the bus depot and the rickshaw was no longer in sight.

I panicked. What was I to do? This was not a North American or European city where I happened to lose merely my traveler's checks. This was one of Asia's most desperate cities, and I was stranded with no identification. I had heard stories of Westerners disappearing in such places, and I was in fear of becoming one of them.

However, I quickly got hold of myself and calmed down. I told myself that in the morning I would go to the Canadian consulate and get a new passport and money. All I had on me now was what was left in my pocket—about seventy rupees, or seven dollars.

I walked back to the hotel where I had stayed. When I told the manager what happened and asked him if I could have a room for the night on credit, he politely said it was impossible. I was not surprised.

I figured my best bet to get through the night would be the first class waiting room in the Howrah train station. The Sealdah or Calcutta train station, where I had been earlier that evening, had a small and crowded waiting room. Howrah's was better. Howrah is the twin city of Calcutta. The two cities are separated by the Hooghly River, a tributary of the Ganges, and are joined by the famous Howrah Bridge which is so often seen in pictures of Calcutta. The Howrah Station is just across the bridge, and is actually the main station for the Howrah-Calcutta metropolis. From the hotel in Calcutta I walked to it in about an hour. I had to conserve what little money I had now, so I didn't take buses.

At the station, the homeless were allowed to stay in the main waiting area, a huge hall which in the daytime would become a frenetic forum of commerce: one would see porters

strenuously running back and forth with trunks and pack-
ages on their heads; vendors selling fruit, vegetables, ready-
made lunches, teas, clothes, sandals, and all sorts of goods;
and trade specialists offering their services to the traveling
public. These specialists would include barbers, tailors, shoe
shiners and cobblers, public letter and document writers and
typists, and even ear cleaners and astrologers. Now, at
night, this commotion had temporarily subsided, yet the station was still full of people. Many of them were sleeping on
the floor. One could tell that most of them weren't waiting
for trains. Indeed, they were Calcutta's homeless. Hungry
and lean, with skin dark from the sun and wrinkled like
leather, and with eyes that stared at the world in silent resignation, they were as forlorn as forlorn could be. The absence
of hope bred by years of suffering was etched in their faces,
and for the most part, there was no need for them to be
theatrical in their begging. Yet for those who did resort to
theater, the extreme limits to which their destitution could
drive them were frightening. A few of them—it was known
to be a fact—purposely maimed their children at birth so they
would better elicit sympathy and alms when they grew older
and begged. These children had knobs for hands, deformed
legs, and eyes burnt out with cigarettes. One came to recognize these children, but one never came to terms with one's
many feelings about them.

The Gentlemen's Waiting Room was set aside from this
main waiting area. Although it was reserved for first class
passengers and one was required to show one's ticket upon
entering, as a foreigner I was not asked any questions by the
watchman. I was exhausted, and immediately fell asleep on
a wooden bench.

❧

Morning arrived, and I walked across the bridge into
Calcutta. I bought myself a tea and a light breakfast, and at
9:00 proceeded to phone the Canadian consulate.

Nobody could provide a phone number for me. After a half hour of trying to find a listing for the Canadian consulate, I decided to call the American consulate. My heart sank when I was informed that there is no Canadian consulate in Calcutta. The nearest Canadian consulate is the embassy (or rather high commission) in New Delhi, eight hundred miles from Calcutta. The American consulate advised me to call the British deputy high commission—that is, consulate—for as a Canadian, I am a British subject; there was nothing more the Americans could do for me.

I decided not to call the British consulate, but to go there in person. It is harder to reject a body than a voice. The trek to the British consulate was harrowing. It took two hours. I tried to ride the buses by squeezing between bodies in the aisle or the back door exit, but the conductor would always find me out and ask for the fare. Though it was not much, I did not want to spend what little I had on busfare; I needed my money for food. So I was thrown off the buses and walked. By 11:00, the sun was high and its rays pounded the pavement. I could see the heat waves radiating as I looked down Chowringhee Road, the main boulevard of downtown Calcutta. The air was sultry and polluted, and a yellow, steamy haze enveloped the city. My feet were in pain. I had thrown my defunct sandals away and, like millions of Indians, was barefoot. But the soles of my feet were soft and sensitive and could not endure the hot pavement. If I had to stand at a corner waiting for a red light, I had to constantly hop from one foot to the other—so hot was the cement. The turning point came when I had to cross a tar-paved intersection. After a dozen steps, it felt as if my feet were on fire. I had to turn around and run back to the corner. As I looked again across the intersection, I could see my footprints branded into the gummy, black tar. My soles red and blistering, I had to buy shoes. Ten rupees went toward a pair of rubber beach thongs.

When I arrived at the consulate, weary and drenched in perspiration, I was seen by a British lady at a reception desk. I explained my emergency situation. After making a brief phone call, she told me that the head of the consular section, a Mr. Graham, would see me shortly.

The consulate was of mildly ornate European architecture, on a quiet street off a main artery. It was large, but not as large as I had expected. The gardens on the grounds were tasteful and well-kept. A big fan turned overhead in the waiting room, and I sat in a leather upholstered chair attempting to gather my composure.

Mr. Graham called me to his office, one story above. He was a middle-aged man, tall and fair. He wore what resembled a British military costume—khaki shirt and shorts, with long socks up to his knees. He sat behind a large, glass-topped, oak desk, and I took a chair facing him. I explained to him my predicament and the problem regarding the Canadian embassy. He took down important identifying information and said he would immediately wire the embassy in New Delhi. We would have to wait for a reply. I thanked him, and then told him that I was almost out of money and had no place to sleep. He suggested that I try the station again. As for money, he was not authorized to give me any, and I would have to make do. He told me to phone him the next day, as he hoped he would then have news for me from the Canadian embassy. I thanked him again and said goodbye.

I wasn't overwhelmed by the consulate's response, but I wasn't complaining either. After all, I was not British, and what could I expect? This was Calcutta. I was grateful for the help and hopeful that my embassy in New Delhi would by the next day authorize or ask the British consulate to advance me some money. Until then, indeed, I would have to make do.

I went to the bank to inform the officer there of my situation, and to see if there was a way to get an advance on the money being wired. Unfortunately, there was nothing he could do. I expressed the urgency of my situation and asked some subtly hinting questions to indicate my knowledge of the rumored Indian bank practices. He said as soon as the money arrived it would be available to me, and I should check with him in a few days.

After leaving Barclays I checked out a few other foreign banks in the area. None used my Canadian bank's intermediary agent and thus to send a new request would be pointless. In any event, without a passport or identification I could initiate no new transaction. Phoning Canada would also be pointless—it would take at least six hours for a call to get through, not to mention the fact that one would not even be heard because of the poor connection—and what could be done that hasn't already been done? The only direct route to send money would be from one American Express office to another. However, I had heard from other travelers who used the American Express office in Calcutta—apparently also run by Indian management—that they too had experienced long delays in receiving money. It seemed there was little I could do but wait.

Following this, I went to the hotel where I had stayed. I slipped by the manager and took a shower. The two showers were accessible to all guests.

Night was approaching, and I was hungry. I bought myself a glass of milk and a small potato dish. I had less than five dollars.

At 9:00 I went to the waiting room at Howrah Station. I was falling asleep on the bench when the watchman woke me. "You were here last night," he said in a gruff voice. He was a big man with a stern look on his face. I said I missed my train and had nowhere to stay. He said it was station policy that nobody could stay in the waiting room more than one night, and I'd have to go. I argued with him, but left as he was about to throw me out bodily.

I went to the main waiting area. It was noisy and dirty. Hundreds of people were sprawled on the floor. Cows rummaged about. Those who were obviously traveling were approached by a steady stream of beggars. Some were very old, some were children—yes, including "those" children—and some were lepers. Half-naked men who had no legs and used their arms to pole vault about were scavenging the station for whatever they could find. I felt depressed, but was too tired to go anywhere else. The walking and heat had taken their toll. I found myself a little spot on the floor and rolled out my sheet and blanket. At least I still had a few comforts. There were people all around me, many of them sleeping with newspapers on them as blankets. I slept poorly, often waking up.

✼

At 7:00 in the morning I packed my bag. The station was beginning to bustle. I noticed that some of the people under the newspapers hadn't moved. They were completely covered, and I wondered if they were all right. I went over to one of them and asked in my simple, colloquial Hindi if everything was okay. No answer, no movement. I lifted off the newspaper and, in utter shock, saw a decomposing body. The flies whizzed about and the stench rose and hit me like a freight train. I let out a holler. People looked at me as if I were deranged. These were all dead bodies under the newspapers.

I left the station. I was in no mood for breakfast, and went to the Maidan, a 1300-acre park off Chowringhee in the central part of Calcutta. I sat under a tree and just rested. Waited. There was, again, not much I could do.

In the afternoon I called Mr. Graham. He said that he received a telegram from the Canadian embassy in New Delhi, informing him that they had wired my family in Canada to send my birth certificate to New Delhi so I could be issued a new passport. I imagined my family's reaction to the news of my situation in Calcutta. Mr. Graham said that I would have to get my money from the bank and then go to

New Delhi. I exclaimed that it could be days before the money arrived, and that the situation was worsening. He said he would see what he could do, and to call him the next day.

Nighttime came again. I could not stay in the Maidan, for at night it became dangerous. Also, the police patrolled the park and prohibited people from sleeping there.

I could not bring myself to go to the Howrah Station. I had an idea. I noticed earlier walking over the Howrah Bridge that on the Calcutta side, underneath the bridge, there were some open spaces near the water. I would go there.

I made my way through the narrow, mazelike streets, using the towering bridge as my guidepost. The Howrah Bridge is a truly magnificent structure. With its modern design and elaborate arches it somewhat resembles the Golden Gate Bridge. It is a huge bridge with six lanes for traffic and a daily commerce that makes it one of the most traveled bridges in the world. All kinds of traffic may be seen crossing it, including pedestrians, bicycles, oxcarts, cows, and buffalos. At night, people sleep on it. In the day, the sun's intense heat supposedly expands its metal to such a degree that it is four cubic feet larger than at night.

The neighborhood I wandered into was a district in its own right, known as Hooghly. It was densely populated, with many of the inhabitants living in bustees—mud and straw huts with no electricity, running water, or sewage system. Most were a few square feet and housed an entire family. People used chulas—small portable stoves—to cook their food, which might consist of some rice, chapati bread, and a few vegetables each day. These people worked in the jute, steel, textile, and other factories of Calcutta, in its railway yards, and in its port. The bustees were huddled closely together, many of them connected by ropes with clothes hanging on them. This was of course to dry the river-washed clothes but also to provide privacy.

There were some shops in this shantytown, as well as some small, open-air temples where I saw Hindus adorning their statue-gods with flowers and praying. Here they worshiped, above all, Kali, the goddess who represents the creative and destructive principles of nature and after whom it is believed Calcutta was named. Sweet incense was thick in the air, and the cacophony of people milling about, bicyclists shouting their way through the crowd, and dogs barking was overwhelming. As I was crossing a street, some people ran by me and a man in their company nearly knocked me down. He obviously did not belong here, as he was dressed like a middle-class Indian. He seemed intoxicated, probably from having just emerged from one of the many opium dens that are hidden away in these neighborhoods. He began to profusely apologize for bumping into me, and before I could understand what had transpired he had squeezed a ten-rupee note into my hand, bowed to me as if I were a *saddhu*, and disappeared.

Saddhus are wandering holy men that may be seen all over India. Many of them travel alone, some in tribes. They have no particular income-earning skills; their vocation is to be holy and to spread holiness throughout the land. They are poor, living only from the alms people give them. It is considered a blessing or a good deed to give money to a *saddhu*. Evidently, this man thought I was a *saddhu*. It was true that I was bearded, as *saddhus* are, but this had never happened before. I was concerned that my appearance was becoming so disheveled that I was beginning to blend into the fabric of India's wandering poor. I also did not feel comfortable having joined the ranks of India's alms recipients. On the other hand, I had to admit that the ten rupees were much needed.

⁂

It was dark by the time I reached the riverbank under the bridge. The gently sloping bank was made of old, cracked

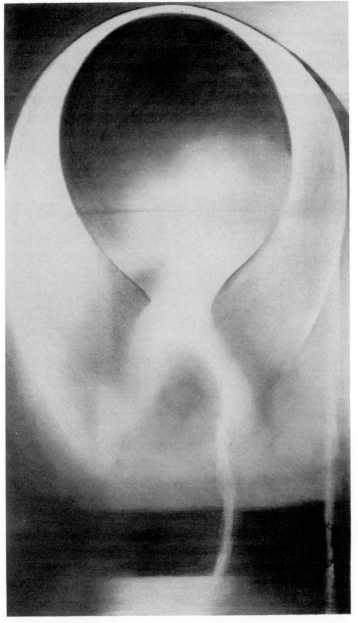

Figure 10. The sur-real, not only in the sense of that which is above or beyond the real, but behind it. Derrick Fludd, *Tear of the Spirit*, New York, 1990. Used by permission.

cobblestones. The open area I was looking for was directly under the bridge. I sat down. I was alone. The water was about six feet away from me. I immediately felt a refreshing, cool breeze bathe me; it was coming up the river from the south. I realized that the river formed a wind tunnel, for it was the only wide open area in the airtight Calcutta-Howrah metropolis. It had been a long time since I had experienced the pleasure of such a wind. It must have been blowing thirty miles per hour. As I let go to its soothing effect, I drifted into a deep relaxation.

After a few moments, I noticed the breeze was not alone in its soothing effort. Above me the concrete mass of the bridge beamed forward towards Howrah. Up till now its hypnotic sound had been subliminal. A deep rumbling emanated from it, from the buses, trucks, and cars that traveled across it. It was not a mechanical sound, but like the rumbling of thunder. It had a peaceful, rhythmic monotony that was all-enveloping. I was mesmerized; I felt that I had entered a kind of surrealistic painting. Looking toward the sky, I saw that the moon had lit up the clouds that were gathered over the river. These billowy clouds were blowing up the river at a speed that seemed to correspond to the flow of the water. The water and clouds seemed connected. The clouds were so low that they seemed to scrape the top of the bridge; it was as if a blanket were being stretched over the river. All this movement somehow seemed to be in perfect rhythm with the rolling thunder above and all around me. The sensation of the breeze brushing across my face, syncopated with the clouds sweeping across the sky and the flowing water and the melodious rumbling, gave the impression that all this was a concerted effort of merging magic. Here in the midst of Calcutta was an astounding mix of natural and manmade beauty. I let my senses indulge in a momentary escape from the grueling sights of the city, in a meditation upon this animated dance between the city and nature. The moon, the clouds, the wind, the dark river, the gurgle of trickling waves a few feet from me, the thunder of the bridge and its vibrations coming through the earth into my body, all seemed so perfect and tranquil. I felt transported into a dreamy world of thoughts. And I began to think.

It seemed to me that I had little control over what was happening to me. Usually when life inflicts a trying situation, it also presents at least a couple of options as to how we may alleviate or overcome it. Here I seemed to have no options. There was no Canadian consulate in Calcutta; I could not expedite the transfer of money from my Canadian bank to the bank in Calcutta; and there were very few social service organizations such as the Red Cross or Peace Corps operating in Calcutta (and certainly none whose priority was to help stranded foreigners). It seemed as if I was doing everything I could to help myself. The rest was in God's hands. How I would end up, in a sense, need be no concern of mine, for there was little I could do about it anyway. If I should not be able to acquire money and a passport soon and harm should come to me, what could I do? I simply had to resign myself to this fact: my life was on "automatic." All I could do aside from what I was already doing was sit back and enjoy the ride—for better or worse. *"Thy will be done."* This realization had an unburdening, peaceful quality, and its truth seemed to be voiced in the larger Gestalt that I was enjoying under this bridge.

Suddenly a man appeared before me, abruptly ending my reverie. He must have come from one of the *bustees* nearby. He was staring at me in a quizzical manner. He was about five-and-a-half feet tall, very lean, dark-complexioned, middle-aged, and dressed in a dirtied *dhoti* and work shirt. I imagined he was a laborer of some sort. The man asked me if I was a *saddhu*. I said no. It occurred to me that to the people of this neighborhood I may have appeared to be a *saddhu* simply because they rarely saw one and, given my foreign, bearded appearance, they didn't know where else to place me in Indian society. Again the man asked if I was a *saddhu*. I said no, I am a foreigner. He didn't understand me. He approached and sat down in front of me. He was gawking at me as if I were from out of this world. He started speaking, but I understood nothing in the Bengali dialect. He then began to prostrate himself at my feet, bowing up and down. Obviously, he was convinced that I was a holy man. Unable to hold my laughter back, I realized how humorless the last two days had been. It felt good to laugh. I again insisted that I was not a *saddhu*, but the man continued his ritual behavior. He was worshiping me as if I were a god. I suppose this might not have been so annoying in and of itself were he not also trying to touch my feet and clasp them. Finally I decided that the only way to put an end to this was to shout at him and scare him off.

After the man had gone I laid down and tried to fall asleep. An hour must have gone by when I noticed two men some twenty feet away, watching me and whispering to each other. These men did not look so placid and reverent as my former admirer. I sensed danger. I got up to leave. One of the men shouted something at me. They approached me. Before anything could happen, I pointed to myself and shouted "*Saddhu! Saddhu!*" This seemed to momentarily put the fear of God into them, as they stopped in their tracks. I hastily disappeared.

Ten minutes later I was walking across the Howrah Bridge, resigned to my fate of spending the night in the Howrah Station. It would at least be safe. As I was crossing, I saw two policemen walking toward me from the other direction. I was afraid they might stop and question me, and possibly even arrest me. It was late at night, and again, these were volatile times. I had no money, no passport or identification, and no place to stay. These factors aside, the police were rumored to be more corrupt than the banks, and false charges brought against foreigners in order to obtain bribes were not uncommon. I did not want any trouble with the police. If Calcutta was hell-on-earth, one could imagine what its jails were like. I turned around before they noticed me and went back into the Hooghly neighborhood from which I had just come. I felt caught between Scylla and Charybdis.

⁂

Throughout this last experience I stayed rather calm. I think that as a result of my wandering thoughts under the bridge, my perception shifted to the back seat and I was simply observing the ride, for better or worse. There was nothing anymore to panic about, nothing to be in control over, nothing to fear.

At a small restaurant-tea shop that was open late, I sat down and had a tea. I figured I'd wait a half hour and then try to cross the bridge again. A young Indian man in Western clothes came over and asked me in perfect English if he could join me. I said fine. He introduced himself as Thanikal. In the course of our conversation he asked what I was doing here so late, and I told him. He said that if I needed a place to sleep that was free and safe, I could go with him; he was in a similar predicament and knew such a place. I asked him about it and all he said was, "Don't worry. Trust me. You'll be safe." He said we would have to wait twenty minutes for a friend of his to join us. He seemed like a decent fellow and I decided to wait and see what would emerge.

The friend shortly arrived and was introduced to me as Bansi. Bansi was in his 20s, fluent in English, and though also obviously middle-class was dressed in a traditional *dhoti*. After Bansi sat down, he began with great emotional intensity to tell us of his problem. He said his brother was in deep trouble and he, Bansi, was doing everything he could to help. The brother was a nuclear physicist and was hiding from the secret police for having stolen classified information from a nuclear plant where he worked. I suppose I listened with some curiosity because the Canadian government's sale of two Candu nuclear reactors to India had recently been a news item in the Canadian press.

Bansi then added that Pakistani agents had infiltrated the plant and his brother had stolen the classified documents before they could get them. The Pakistanis wanted to build a bomb and it was imperative that the Indians build one first (it was not long after the 1971 Indo-Pakistani War). The brother was holding onto the documents until he could be sure that the authorities he gave them to were the correct ones, as he also suspected the police of being infiltrated by Pakistani agents. A good look into Bansi's eyes at this point confirmed what his story implied: he was psychotic. His eyes had a look of madness, of a desperate, lost soul. I looked over to Thanikal: his face had an expression of familiarity, as if he had heard this story before. Yet there was no judgment in this expression, and I could not tell whether or not Thanikal was part of the "plot." Thanikal looked at me and probably saw the concern in my facial expression. He humoringly said, "Don't worry about him."

I was hesitant to go anywhere with these characters. They seemed harmless enough, but this did not mean they were not an invitation to danger. One of them was certainly so deluded and paranoid that it was impossible to predict his actions. On the other hand, it might be a few more days before my money would arrive, and a free, safe place to stay would be a great asset. I again tried to elicit information from Thanikal: was this place we were going to a public service of some sort, a hostel, a temple or church? All he said was, "Trust me. It's better than the station."

"Oh what-the-hell," I thought to myself. I may as well go along for the ride—for better or worse.

We started out on foot in an easterly direction, but I soon lost track of where we were going. The streets were dark, and we turned so many corners that I had no idea which part of the city we were in. We walked at a brisk pace for well over an hour. I was becoming more tired with each moment. Even my light shoulder bag seemed heavy. Fortunately, it was night and the temperature was only in the 80s. Thanikal was of course leading the way, as Bansi was quite disoriented. Bansi talked incessantly; by now the Russians and Chinese had become embroiled in his nuclear drama.

Finally we turned a corner and walked down a street, and it seemed we had entered another world. We walked into a wide open area that appeared to be a dilapidated park. It stretched at least four blocks. There were hundreds of people, many awake, many sleeping wherever they could. There was something strange about this place, these people, but I couldn't put my finger on it.

Suddenly a man ran toward us. He had a crazed look on his face, and his eyes were bulging out of his head. His hair and beard were long and unkempt. He was completely naked. His hand was clasping his penis. Aghast, I stared at him. He shouted something at us of which I understood not one word, and then he ran by us. I looked at Thanikal. He looked at me and said in his by-now familiar, humoring way, "Don't worry. He's always here."

I could feel the tension building in my neck. I had difficulty swallowing. I couldn't believe my eyes. Everybody here was crazy! This was the "caste of the insane."

In India, there are innumerable castes or colonies. It is a misconception that India has wiped out its caste system. In Bombay, I had observed the so-called "untouchables" living in cordoned-off sections that were actually construction worksites. Entire colonies were hired—at unconscionable wages—by construction companies to build the large office buildings of expanding foreign corporations. Men, women, and children worked round-the-clock shifts in conditions that were subhuman, or at best, what one would imagine to be typical of the Industrial Revolution. The children did not attend school. Undernourished, barely clothed and shielded from the sun, everybody worked, of all ages. When one job was over, the colony would pick up and move to another. Throughout India I saw castes like these—leper castes, castes of the disabled, and simply poor, non-landowning castes that inherit their alienating legacy from one generation to the next. Of course, there are some castes that are better off than others, such as the occupational castes of Calcutta. The potters' caste and conch-shell workers' caste, for example, have their own districts, and the names of the districts reflect the occupational trades which are the heirlooms and trademarks of these castes.

However, here I had stumbled into one of the least fortunate castes, the caste of the mentally disturbed. Most likely it also included the mentally retarded, who because of neglect or abuse probably developed disturbances in addition to their given handicaps. They would thus not be particularly distinguishable from the others. India by and large does not have the resources or professional services to maintain institutions for the mentally disturbed and retarded. They go untreated, and join together in bands and colonies that either wander the countryside or are hidden in obscure neighborhoods in India's inner cities. Up till now I had only heard about these "tribes" through rumor. Like with *saddhus*, who of course are far more visible, it is considered a good deed to give alms to the mentally disturbed, many of whom are beggars. I imagined that this Calcutta caste lived off the generosity of restaurants and other businesses. Certainly, their living conditions could not have been worse than in some of the institutions that are still in operation in the more affluent Western nations.

Nevertheless, this sight was a horror. The mentally ill often do not attend to their physical hygiene. This tendency combined with the lack of facilities available to these people predisposes them to a deterioration of the body that one cannot imagine. Add to this the self-destructive impulses common to certain disorders, and one truly has a picture of the wretched of the earth.

I saw a lady who was emaciated and walking around in a dazed state. The rag she wore for a dress had a large hole around her belly, and the skin of the belly was red and

Figure 11. The infernal city, being built by devils and humans alike. In the background is a fiery, red sky. Hieronymus Bosch, *The Hay Wain Triptych* (detail), 1490–1500. Monastery of San Lorenzo, Escorial, Spain.

chapped. She kept rubbing it in a circular motion and seemed to be repeating something monotonously under her breath. Perhaps she had been raped, or had lost a baby, or was obsessed with pregnancy fantasies. Or perhaps she was simply hungry—very hungry. Another woman, naked from the waist up, had skin like a raisin withered in the sun. There were big holes in her ear lobes, from which hung long, heavy earrings. A heavy ring hung from the side of her nose. The nipples of her breasts must have been pierced too: big rings hung from them as well. One word came repeatedly out of her mouth in a shrill and haunting voice: "Kali! Kali! Kali!" Was this the demon who possessed her? Dozens sat about on the ground, rocking back and forth in a regressed state, staring into the unknown. Some were engaged in lively conversations with what were probably imaginary voices, to them real and terrifying. No doubt, most of these people were schizophrenic. Without medication and treatment, their pathology was free to reign in its most raw and aberrant forms. Without medication and treatment, they had no hope.

I knew now why Thanikal had said this place would be safe: no thieves would come here. What could they steal? I also knew why it was free.

Should I stay or should I go? It was a long way back to the station, and I didn't even know how to get there. It was two or three in the morning; I was exhausted. Although I was in an insane environment, I did not sense danger: these people were harmful to themselves, not others. Curiously, in spite of the intense isolation each of them must have felt in their chaotic inner worlds, they managed to maintain a loose sense of community and belonging with each other. These people stayed together. And, of considerable importance to me at this moment, they did not seem to mind my presence. In fact, they did not even take notice of it. Thus, when Thanikal said, "Come along, we'll find a place to lie down," I went. When we found a spot, I put my thongs under my bag and my bag under my head, and I went out like a light.

☙

The sun woke me in the early morning. My body was stiff and not well-rested. People were teeming all about me, their agitated conditions seemingly heating up in the sun. Thanikal was gone. So was Bansi. I lifted up my bag. My thongs were missing; somebody must have pulled them from under my head while I was asleep. I was annoyed, but what could I do? I would have to buy another pair.

With directions from somebody on the street and the aid of a few familiar landmarks, I found my way to Chowringhee Road. I bought myself another pair of thongs, and went to a restaurant for breakfast. I then went to the British consulate. I had to wait before Mr. Graham could see me. Hours went by. Waiting ahead of me was an elegantly dressed, upper-class Indian couple emigrating to England. They were apparently here for final approval of their visas. They looked at me with curiosity. I suppose it was an ironic sight: the opulence of India escaping to the West, sitting opposite a haggard, underweight Westerner trapped in Calcutta.

Finally the Indian couple went to Mr. Graham's office. A half hour passed before they came back. In the waiting area they stopped to ask the receptionist something, and as she was replying her phone rang. She excused herself, picked up the receiver, was on for but a moment, and then turned to me. She announced that Mr. Graham will be taking lunch, after which he has an appointment, and would I be good enough to return this afternoon at 4:30? Now I knew that 4:30 would be close to the end of the official day, and all that Mr. Graham would most probably do would be to give me a few kind words of encouragement and tell me to call tomorrow. But this would be my third day of roaming the streets of Calcutta. My money was running low—dangerously low—

and my body was weary. I was not sleeping or eating well, and the few pounds I had gained since my dysentery episode were now lost. If I were to keep up this pace of walking miles and miles in the city while not adequately nourishing myself, I would continue to lose weight. Compounding this, a nasty heat rash had broken out on my body, and the newspapers had announced a cholera outbreak in the city. Though I had had a vaccine, it was soon due to "expire." The situation was going from bad to worse. Tomorrow would be Friday, and then the weekend. What then?

I politely told the receptionist that this arrangement would not do, and would she ask Mr. Graham to please see me now for a few minutes? The Indian couple looked at me, obviously surprised by my imposing manner. The receptionist more or less repeated what she had already said. I briefly explained my circumstances and the urgency of my situation. She agreed to ask again, picked up the phone, and relayed my request. A moment later she put it down and said I would have to wait till this afternoon.

So this is where the ride was taking me—for better or worse. I was still in the frame of mind which had emerged when I was under the Howrah Bridge: peaceful, calm, resigned to the powers that be, my desperation as exhausted as my body. But I figured that I still had to do all that I could to help myself. And so, although I did not in fact feel naturally inclined toward an emotional display, I realized that now was the time for one.

I gripped the edge of the receptionist's desk with both hands and, in a bellowing voice that I knew would reverberate up into Mr. Graham's office, I started hollering: "Look here! If I go out on those streets for another day I'm going to die! I'm at the end of my rope! Now I've made my situation perfectly clear to you people and all you could say is it's time for tea! Well get this straight: I'm not leaving here till I get help! Do you understand!? You could call the police, I don't give a damn! I'm a Canadian citizen! A British subject! I grew up singing 'God Save Our Gracious Queen' and this is how you treat me!? Despicable! Despicable!" My head was shaking, my eyes were rolling, and if my face looked like it felt I'm sure it was red like a beet. The poor receptionist looked terribly frightened and jumped away from her desk. The Indian couple darted to the other side of the room and were looking at me as if I were a member of the caste whose company I had just left. Terror was in the air.

Mr. Graham, with a host of others behind him, came running down the stairs. He stopped halfway down and, leaning over the bannister, shouted "What's going on!? What's the problem!?" We looked at each other. His eyes registered alarm. The receptionist volunteered that I had said I would not leave until I received help. She continued on about something to the effect that she did not expect me to raise my voice, but Mr. Graham, now noticing the Indian couple and evidently embarrassed, interrupted her. He said, "That's perfectly all right. Mr. Gellert, will you please come to my office?" I followed him up.

Seated opposite from me at his desk, Mr. Graham asked me what the problem was. I explained to him in detail all I had been through since we last spoke. I told him that I was running out of places to stay, that my health was deteriorating, that I was almost out of money. I said I needed help and I needed it now. He listened attentively, and said he had an idea. His friend was director of the Salvation Army in Calcutta, and although it would not provide accommodations for the stranded or homeless whether native of Calcutta or not, he would ask him if an exception could be made in my instance. He couldn't guarantee anything, but he would try. He would reach him this afternoon after lunch and his appointment, and I should call back around 4:30. So, we were back to 4:30, but at least something hopeful was in the works. I thanked Mr. Graham very much and left.

I went to the bank again, but there were no new developments. The officer assured me that by next week the money should be here.

At 4:30 I called Mr. Graham. Good news! I could stay at the Salvation Army until my money arrived. I could eat in its cafeteria on credit, the director would loan me any other funds I needed, and I could pay the sum total before I left. The director was expecting me at 7:00. Mr. Graham gave me the address and directions. I deeply thanked him.

I ate dinner and by 6:00 was on my way to the Salvation Army. When I arrived I was ushered in to the director's office. He was a pleasant man and made me feel very welcome. A bed was provided for me in a large dormitory. The men who stayed here were all "regulars." Most were Indians, some were Anglo-Indians, and a few were from other countries in the Orient. All worked in the city and some had been residents of the Salvation Army for as long as fifteen years. It was not only their home, but as I came to understand, their culture and religion, for the Salvation Army was considered almost as its own Christian denomination. It operated a variety of relief projects in the city, much in line with our ideas of the Salvation Army in North America and Europe.

⁂

The Salvation Army is a fortresslike compound situated in the Muslim quarter of Calcutta. This is a relatively quiet neighborhood with a distinct Islamic flavor. There are a number of small mosques with spiring minarets; from their windows one could hear in the early morning the muezzins sing the traditional Muslim prayer call.

I was at the Salvation Army for two weeks. My money got "lost" somewhere, and it took this long for the bank to trace and retrieve it. In these weeks, I ate well and rested, and gained back a portion of my strength. I borrowed money from the director's office, using some to send a telegram to my family in Canada so they would not worry and some to buy penicillin to treat my rash. I saw Mr. Graham one more time. He had received notification that my documents had arrived at the Canadian embassy in New Delhi. I would have to go there so I could be issued a new passport. Mr. Graham drafted an official letter which would in the meantime serve as a temporary form of identification.

During the two weeks at the Salvation Army, I experienced an unexpected, dramatic change in mood. It is true that the tempo of my life significantly slowed down compared to the days before, and I was able to relax—at least physically. Psychologically, however, my former state of peaceful resignation had passed, and in its place there grew a state of agitation, a peculiar sense of something gnawing at me from inside. It pursued me everywhere I went and in everything I did. It was there when I went to bed and it was there when I awoke. I suppose that with the immediate threat of danger now removed, the weight of what had passed finally began to "sink in." I had been a hair's breadth away from death, and perhaps even closer to joining Calcutta's disenfranchised. But somehow I could not understand—aside from my own standpoint of needed survival—what difference this made. So what if I was spared? Millions—*millions!*—were not.

The insignificance of the fact that I was able to escape Calcutta was borne out not only by the contrasting numbers of those who could not; for when I had wandered among the people in the streets and did not feel far from becoming one of them, I could not distinguish what had formerly made my condition in life—its fundamental quality—so different than their own. If they were the have-nots, what did I have? What was it that I was so driven to re-acquire, thinking that I was at risk of losing it? What was it under the bridge that I no longer feared to lose because something told me that either I never had it to lose in the first place or I could never lose it or it didn't make a difference if I did? Certainly, one thing I had—which the people I saw didn't—was the gift to enjoy life. But this gift existed purely because of the materialistic affluence and opportunities afforded to me by virtue of my birth in a developed country, and now I realized how transitory this gift really was, how life could take it away with one swift blow. And then, what would I "have," what would I "be"?

I suppose also that the spirit of India, and particularly Calcutta, had caught up with me, seizing me in its grip. In its vision of the world, time is measured in *kalpas* or *maha yugas*—eons in which millenia are not even chapters or pages but words, and an individual's life not even a speck. Indeed, time seemed to expand and slow down in India: a day seemed like three, and a week like a month. And one's sense of personal uniqueness—the importance of individual identity which we so strongly cultivate in the West—also seemed to melt into this Indian Sea of infinity, of endless time and peopledness.

Against this background, I could not help but wonder about the significance of my life. What purpose does it serve? Eventually, it and its fruits will be entirely gone, imperceptibly absorbed into this sea. A sense of great uncertainty and disillusionment set in as the value of my past accomplishments and future plans—a value I had always taken for granted—paled. And, in light of this disillusionment, I wondered about God: Is he truly a personal God, intimately involved in our struggles, or is he detached, watching us from an infinite, cosmic vantage point? How does he figure into this world, with its Calcuttas and Holocausts and starving children with burnt-out eyes? Indeed, is there really a God at all? Given the suffering and meaninglessness that so often seem to prevail in life, is he not a product of our imaginations, something we *wish* would exist and therefore create? And what if there is no God, what then does this say about our lives? In a Godless world, what would endure from them, and in Whose eyes?

Clearly, I had become smitten by questions that all come down to that single, burning question which Tolstoy so succinctly summed up as follows: "Is there any meaning in my life that the inevitable death awaiting me does not destroy?"[1] Of course, people have been asking themselves this question, and the others it gives rise to, throughout the ages. They are questions whose answers presuppose absolute knowledge; if nobody has successfully, unequivocally, answered them by now, obviously I was not going to either. Yet like a dark mood that takes possession of one, these questions turned over and over in my mind, and I could not get them out.

On my last day in Calcutta—in fact, as I was packing my bag in preparation to leave and pondering these things—I slipped into a strange state of awareness. There was something vaguely familiar about it, as if I had tasted it in my childhood, yet it seemed far beyond any childhood experience.

Beginning around noon and continuing till the end of the day, the world "looked" and my inner being "felt" entirely different, different than usual, that is. Yet in itself everything seemed perfectly right, perfectly natural. There was nothing really extra-ordinary or out-of-this-world about how I felt, although it was very blissful—indeed, ecstatic. It was the most intense, emotionally powerful experience I had ever had. It was as if an energy were pulsating through my mind and entire nervous system.

The physical world also seemed to have an enhanced, vibrant quality, like in Van Gogh's painting *The Starry Night*. Yet again, to emphasize, there was no outstanding, singular feature—for example, a white light—as people often attribute

---

[1]Leo Tolstoy, *A Confession, The Gospel in Brief, and What I Believe,* translated with an introduction by Aylmer Maude (London: Oxford University Press, 1961), p. 24.

to drug or near-death experiences; I was able to function perfectly well in society. The best way I could describe this state is to say that everything was "one," and everything was perfect in itself. As I walked through the streets of Calcutta, I felt totally at one with everything and everybody. The suffering of children that usually made me shudder, the decrepit look of worn and tattered beggars that always haunted me, the disgusting squalor, ignorance, and noisy confusion plaguing the streets of this infernal city—all seemed part of a perfect process now. It all seemed "right"—not right in contrast to wrong, but right in the sense that things are perfect as they are, that "the universe is unfolding as it should." This is not to undermine free will and social responsibility; it is not to say that certain conditions, e.g., socioeconomics, can't or shouldn't be changed or improved for the better, but rather that life as a whole is perfect as it is.

My statement that I felt at one with everything and everybody probably has cliché connotations by now; it or statements like it have been overused in our culture. Perhaps some elaboration is necessary. One way to describe this oneness is to say that it felt as if the infinite sky were the limit or roof of my mind, and every created thing beneath were my own thoughts. I don't at all mean this egocentrically. Simply, when I looked at the beggars, the women and children, or the smoke coming out of a pot on a fire, there was no difference, or rather, separateness, between what I saw and myself. I did not feel like an outsider, apart from everything. In fact, there was no "I" who felt this way or that way, or who thought this thought and that thought. There was only pure watching, pure attentiveness.

I remember the distinct sensation that occurred at a certain moment when I was walking to the train station and turned a street corner. The trees and greenery of the Maidan came into close view, and the musical chirping of birds pierced through the noise of the city. All of a sudden it seemed as if a veil which had been covering the world had been lifted. The essential animatedness of the trees, green-ery, and chirping birds "leaped out," and it became strikingly clear that this animatedness was *Everything*! In a moment I couldn't tell where it was coming from: it was outside me, it was inside me, it *was me*. The world was bathed in it and radiating it. In the same moment, it seemed as if "the bottom had fallen out" of the universe and the latter had been emp-tied of fixed centers of identity, of the "thingness" of things. The trees just "hung there" in an all-surrounding "net" of vivid hollowness, and yet the trees were of this hollowness and so was I. This emptiness had a most exhilarating and liberating—mentally freeing—quality. It was not a negative or nihilistic emptiness as in the "nothingness" of Sartre and the existentialists, but rather a "pregnant" emptiness. It seemed to go together with the oneness of everything.

Of course, I was still fully cognizant of the suffering of the people I saw everywhere, but I no longer felt the pain of identifying myself or others with it. Yet for those who did identify with their suffering, who seemed to be most every-body I saw, I felt compassion—not pity, or sorrow, or even guilt, as I usually felt, but just compassion. Indeed, the crux of this state was that there was no "I." It seemed as if the "I" who was watching was God who was watching, and the world I was watching was God whom I was watching; everything was God, absolutely everything. In light of this, everything seemed perfect and natural. I felt a complete peace and harmony with the world and inherent *in* the world.

Now when I say "God" here, I am aware that this term may raise some misconceptions. I certainly do not wish to imply an anthropomorphic image of God as "a-wise-old-man-in-the-sky-with-a-long-flowing-white-beard"— although neither do I wish to convey an impression of some-thing altogether nonhuman when one considers *what* it is that makes us human or humane. There was a definite senti-ence to this "God," and my understanding of it at the time was that it is the mind of the universe. But more than the mind: the mind-body-soul. It is the universe itself, but with intelligence—a supreme intelligence. It was as if my mind had for a time fused with this intelligence, and there was no line of separation between us. In fact, my own mind and life, and the intelligence and life of everybody and everything around me, seemed to be equal manifestations or "faces" of this universal intelligence. All were one. This was experienced on a very "crisp," perceptual level; it was not conceptual or abstract.

There are two points I wish to add here. Firstly, it was implicitly clear to me that this intelligence always *was* and always *is* there, or here, and that I had hitherto only been unaware of it, *unconscious* of it. With the shift in my conscious state, this intelligence became ever-so-evident. How could I have never perceived it before? It is *so obvious*, for it permeates everything, everywhere. Thus, the fact that this universal mind appears hidden from us is as much a reflection of our own unconsciousness of it as of its apparently invisible, intangible quality. If our own minds and lives are indeed manifestations of it, then it is the foundation of who we are. It is our innermost nature, our unconscious self at its deepest or highest level. It also became plainly evident that, being the universal mind, this unconscious self is eternal. I felt during these hours that I was standing under the umbrella of Eternity, that regardless of the torrents of rain that might fall on me during this life, the "I-less I" who was watching all this would live forever. Perhaps it is this essence that gets reincarnated, or certainly, if reincarnation doesn't exist, this that continues to survive in some other realm, in some other form. Whatever else would endure from personal identity—such as the soul or karma—I could not conjecture, but I intuitively knew that the purpose of our lives here is to express the intelligence and will of this universal mind as much as we could. *We* are the still good hand of God.

This brings me to my second and perhaps most important point. This intelligence emanated not only incredible energy but incredible compassion—a benevolent concern for all that is. Perhaps this is what the religious sages of old meant by divine love—and, I suppose like them, I too could not help but be raptured by and wrapped up in it. It was far more intense and "immediate" than any other love I had ever experienced, and yet it had a most gentle quality to it. It transformed Calcutta before my eyes. Whatever the grand purpose of life may be, it became clear to me that it has much to do with learning to love with such a depth and capacity. This is not to raise the world to God's level, or even to see the world *as* God. Rather, it is to see the world *as it is*.

Perhaps to be expected, I did not analyze any of this until much later. At the time there was nothing to analyze. I went to bed that night completely exhausted, as if the effort to maintain the state of awareness I was in was more than I was accustomed to. Little did I know that the next morning I would awaken in my usual state—my regular, old self—except for one difference: the knowledge of having had this experience. Its impact upon me has lasted to this day.

&

In a nonintellectual way, this experience resolved the questions, doubts, and disillusionment which had taken hold of me. It became clear to me that our true nature, and consequently our place in the world, are much more than we ordinarily think. Of course, we are still transitory beings— "from ashes to ashes, dust to dust"—but everything in this experience seemed to point to the notion that what is transitory is our conscious identity. Our unconscious seems to be the part of us that was created in God's image—transcendent and eternal. The unconscious, at root, seems to be the spirit or consciousness of God himself. This would imply a dramatic shift in meaning of the term "unconscious." For according to this notion, the unconscious is *very* conscious, and it is *we* who are unconscious—un-conscious of *it*. As Emerson wrote, "There is an important *équivoque* in our use of the word Unconscious, a word which is much displayed upon in the psychology of the present day. . . . But the unconsciousness we spake of was merely relative to *us*. . . . we predicate nothing of its consciousness or unconsciousness in relation to itself."[2] This same shift is reflected in the Taoist parable of the disciple who tells his master of a dream he had of a butterfly. The master retorts, "How do you know you are not now a butterfly dreaming that you are a man?"

Experiences of the kind I had are not uncommon, especially in the mystical traditions that have thrived at one time or another in most religions. They have also been a topic of discussion in a number of psychology and other contemporary books.[3] What emerges in a review of such experiences is that most of them are preceded by an emotionally and psychologically turbulent period which involves an assault upon one's basic perception of the world. This assault usually takes the form of some trauma or disturbing experience that unloosens the ego's strong hold on reality as we know it. If the ego is fragile or unstable to begin with, this may result in a serious depression; at worst, it may lead to a nervous (i.e., emotional) breakdown or even a psychotic episode. However, if the ego is sufficiently well-developed and stable, it can safely endure the transformation that takes place. Most mystical traditions foster this assault and transformation

---

[2]Ralph Waldo Emerson, *Emerson in His Journals*, selected and edited by Joel Porte (Cambridge, MA: Belknap Press of Harvard University Press, 1982), p. 237 (entry of April 27–29, 1840).

[3]Some especially good ones, to mention only a few, include: William James, *The Varieties of Religious Experience* (1902; 1985) Richard Maurice Bucke, *Cosmic Consciousness* (1901; 1969); Evelyn Underhill, *Mysticism* (1911; 1955); Raynor Johnson, *Watcher on the Hills* (1959); Abraham Maslow, *Religion, Values and Peak Experiences* (1964) and *Toward a Psychology of Being* (1968); and Charles Tart (ed.), *Altered States of Consciousness* (1969).

through safe, disciplined methods (e.g., contemplative prayer, meditation, etc.) Yet even these are often not without turbulent, disturbing features. For the nature of the transformation is itself painful: it requires the ego to "let go" of its sovereign position in the driver's seat and to take a position in the back seat—to let the unconscious emerge and to see through its eyes, or, if you prefer, the eyes of God.

"Letting go" is not easy, though by the sound of the words, it should be. Certainly, it is contrary to all our conditioning and values, which is one reason why many mystical traditions have had a secret or underground status within their religions. Yet a careful examination of the main bodies of literature of these religions will reveal that they are expli-

Figure 12. Jonah emerging from the belly of the whale. Jan Brueghel, *Oel auf Holz*, late 16th or early 17th century. Alte Pinakothek, Munich. Used by permission.

citly (even if symbolically) concerned with this psychological, mystical transformation. One may immediately think of the Exodus of the Israelites from the Egyptian "House of Bondage." Their forty-year pilgrimage through the desert in order to "un-learn" their former values was necessary before they could enter the "Promised Land." Christ, too, spent forty days in the desert – being tempted by the devil – before he began his ministry. Buddha's transformative journey before he attained enlightenment was ridden with questions on the nature of suffering and the meaning of life; Zen Buddhists call such intense questioning the "Great Doubt." St. John of the Cross described his period of trials and tribulations as the "dark night of the soul." And finally, the prophet Jonah experienced his "dark night" in the belly of a whale. Ignoring God's command to go to the sinful people of Nineveh and teach them of God's ways, Jonah had run off with some sailors to sea. When he was subsequently thrown into the sea during a storm, God arranged for a whale to swallow him. Here, in the "belly of hell," he was forced to let go of his obstinate ways and to recognize the will of God: even a city as wicked as Nineveh was not to be excluded from God's love and redemption.

In this chapter, I have described my visit to Calcutta in some detail. Much of this visit turned out to be a gradual but accumulative assault upon not only my senses but my emotional and psychological sensibilities: things just stopped making sense the way they normally did. From this emerged a new perspective. However, one does not have to go to Calcutta or some other exotic place for this to happen. I have seen people undergo such changes in more ordinary circumstances. It is the inner, spiritual inquisitiveness that is the crucial ingredient, and not the external factors. The belly of the whale is really not a place, but a state of mind.

CHAPTER 5

LILA: THE SPORT OF GOD

In Tennessee Williams' *A Streetcar Named Desire*, Blanche says to Mitch, at a moment when he is embracing her and she feels herself falling in love, "Sometimes there's God so quickly." Indeed, sometimes there's God so quickly. If God somehow resides in the innermost core of our unconscious minds, as suggested in the preceding chapter, then it goes without saying that he is never far from us and can break through into our conscious minds at any time, giving us a glimpse of the world as he sees it. In this chapter, I would like to discuss the process which is at the root of such a breakthrough. In relation to this, I also wish to look at how the mind of God might fit into the scheme of our psyches, or rather, how our psyches might fit into the scheme of God's mind.

᪣

In the mystical traditions of all the major world religions, there have evolved disciplines that attempt to cultivate a state of mind in which the *mysterium tremendum* can manifest and flourish. In Western religions, the predominant discipline has been prayer—not verbal prayer in which one is asking God for blessings, but contemplative prayer in which one sinks into an awareness only of God's presence. In Eastern religions, the predominant discipline has been meditation. Though there are many schools and methods, their aims tend to be similar: to transcend the limitations of ego-consciousness and allow a deeper consciousness—a consciousness of the Absolute (regardless of which name it is known by)—to emerge. There has been much written on the disciplines of prayer and meditation. If dreams are the royal road to the unconscious, as Freud asserted, then it seems that prayer and meditation are the royal roads to the *mysterium tremendum*.

However, both Western and Eastern mystics have discovered that their disciplines are not fixed to any particular formulas, that they are not rigid *things* but rather active *processes* that reflect a state of mind, an attitude, if you wish. Hence, it becomes possible to exercise a prayerful or meditative attitude in *anything*—in any discipline—that we choose to practice. This is fortunate for people who for one reason or another do not like formal prayer or meditation. This possibility permits people, such as the 17th-century Christian mystic Brother Lawrence, to discover God while working in the monastery kitchen or repairing shoes; it allows Zen masters to experience the Tao through the disciplines of calligraphy, tea ceremony, pottery making, bamboo flute music, or whatever other forms of expression may be preferred. Apparently, it is less important *what* the discipline is than what the *quality of discipline* invested into it is. If the quality of discipline—of concentration or what the Zen Buddhists call one-pointedness of mind—is strong enough, pure enough, and sustained for long enough, we become so absorbed in the activity that the usual boundaries of the ego become extended. If they become extended enough, there comes a moment when we merge not only with the activity outside of us, but with the unconscious within. (The breaking through of the unconscious thus goes hand-in-hand, once again, with a letting go of the ego.) It is in this way that we can have a religious experience while engaged in some meaningful or involving activity, seeing the activity through the eyes of God and God through the activity.

This process is what the Hindus call *lila*. A Sanskrit word, it means "sport" and refers to the recreational game of the god Vishnu, the Creator. *Lila* is God playing or exercising himself in creation, in the world of forms. The film actor Alan Arkin provides an illustration of an experience of *lila*, and in doing so, highlights another dimension of the genius factor. He is here describing an occurrence that took place during the third performance of a play he was directing:

> On the third night something extraordinary happened. I sat in the back of the theater, watching from my usual place, and as the lights came up I could see the actors were not doing what I had directed. With each entrance, something unexpected was taking place. Gestures changed, placement on the stage, timing and energy level were all different. I am a strong director and have a very definite idea of how a play should go, and my initial reaction was that my work was being willfully subverted. But as the play went on, I could begin to see that what was happening was unconscious on the part of the actors, and had infected all sixteen of them uniformly. The play had taken on a life of its own, independent of anything I had desired, and also independent of the actors' desires. I sat for two-and-a-half hours watching this event as if I had never seen it before. After the play I went backstage to talk to the actors. I wanted to tell them what I had witnessed, but as we came together I could see in their faces that they knew. It was impossible to say anything. No words came out of my mouth. No one else could speak. We remained together, standing motionless for minutes, all of us silently sharing this sense of awe and joy. It was an enormous act of will to finally break apart

and go our separate ways, and it was an experience none of us will ever forget.

The run proceeded smoothly and the empathy and energy continued, though nothing like that one performance ever quite happened again.[1]

More explicitly, we see the occurrence of *lila* in the experiences of athletes who are actually engaged in sports. Michael Murphy and Rhea White write that an athlete who has a mystical experience through his sport "knows that being in perfect control of the football, or the puck, or the bat may be a matter more of grace than of will, and that one can only 'do it' by letting it happen, by letting something else take over, as it were."[2] One is given the impression that "something else" is "taking over" in the enchanting baseball story by Bernard Malamud, *The Natural*. But such stories are not entirely fictitious, for the history of sports is full of them. Basketball player Patsy Neal offers a poignant account of her experience competing in the Free-Throw Championship at the National Amateur Athletic Union Basketball Tournament. She had been preparing rigorously for the event but because of all the spectators present was too nervous to perform well in the early rounds of the competition. Feeling a sense of doom, she prayed for help before going to bed the night before the final round. And then:

> . . . a strange thing happened in my sleep. Sometime during the night, I had a dream. I was shooting the free-throws, and each time the ball fell through the goal, the net would change to the image of Christ. It was as though *I* was flowing into the basket instead

---

[1] Alan Arkin, *Halfway Through the Door: An Actor's Journey Toward the Self* (New York: Harper & Row, 1981), pp. 94–95. Copyright © 1979 by Alan Arkin. Reprinted by permission of Alan Arkin.

[2] Michael Murphy and Rhea A. White, *The Psychic Side of Sports* (Reading, MA: Addison-Wesley, 1978), p. 32.

of the ball. I felt endless, unhampered . . . and in some way I was connected to the image of Christ that kept flowing from the basket. The sensation was that of transcending *everything*. I was more than I was. I was a particle flowing into *all* of life. It seems almost profane to try to describe the feeling because words are so very inadequate.

The next day, I still had the feeling when I woke. I felt as though I was *floating* through the day, not just living it. That evening, when I shot my free-throws in the finals, I was probably the calmest I have ever been in my life. I didn't . . . see or hear the crowd. It was only me, the ball, and the basket. The number of baskets I made really had no sense of importance to me at the time. The only thing that really mattered was what I *felt*. But even so, I would have found it hard to miss even if I had wanted to.

. . . I know now what people mean when they speak of a "state of grace." I was in a state of grace, and if it were in my power to maintain what I was experiencing at that point in time, I would have given up everything in my possession in preference to that sensation.[3]

Scoring forty-eight baskets out of fifty, Neal won the championship.

The heightened state of consciousness which Neal describes as a "state of grace" and as "transcending *everything*" seems to also transcend the sequential structure of time. David Meggyesey, a former football player with the St. Louis Cardinals, admitted that in a particular game in which he played brilliantly he fell into "a kind of trance where I could sense the movements of the running backs a split sec-

---

[3]Patsy Neal, *Sport and Identity*, also cited in Michael Murphy and Rhea A. White, *op. cit.*, pp. 133–34.

ond before they happened."[4] This trancelike awareness is actually cultivated in the Japanese martial arts. The Zen influence on these arts, especially *kendo* or swordsmanship, is notable. Japan's *kendo* masters are not being facetious when they claim they can sense every movement their opponents are going to make and intuitively know when and how to strike them.[5] (The *Star Wars* movies are very much based on the Samurai tradition of *kendo*. The "Force" which is so celebrated in these movies as the guiding spirit that helps the "Jedi warrior" fight flawlessly is no other than the force of the unconscious.)

In a similar way are the usual operations of space transcended. In his book about his years of arduous training with a Japanese archery master, Eugen Herrigel recounts an incident in which his master told him that he hits the target without using his eyes. When Herrigel scoffed at this, the master, to prove his point, allowed Herrigel to set up the target in a practice hall that was brightly lit but in which the target area was pitch-black, thus making it impossible for one's vision to adjust to the darkness and delineate the target. Herrigel writes: "[The master's] first arrow shot out of dazzling brightness into deep night. I knew from the sound that it had hit the target. The second arrow was a hit, too. When I switched on the light in the target-stand, I discovered to my amazement that the first arrow was lodged full in the middle of the black [bull's-eye], while the second arrow had splintered the butt of the first and plowed through the shaft before embedding itself beside it." Explaining his precision, the master said, "It is not 'I' who must be given credit for this shot. 'It' shot and 'It' made the hit."[6] Of course, the true goal of any martial art practiced in the Zen spirit it not to

---

[4]Cited in Michael Murphy and Rhea A. White, *op. cit.*, p. 137.
[5]Michael Murphy and Rhea A. White, *ibid*.
[6]Eugen Herrigel, *Zen in the Art of Archery* (New York: Vintage Books, Random House, 1971), pp. 84–85.

achieve spectacular feats but to attune oneself to the unconscious mind, to "It"; winning against one's opponent or hit-
ting the target is only a by-product of this inner
attunement.[7]

🎜

The idea of *lila* takes on a special twist when one considers that there is, as the Hindus believe, a more subtle
sport going on within any particular form of sporting that
God chooses to exercise through. And that is the sport or
game of hide-and-go-seek. God appears and then disap-
pears. Where did he come from, where did he go? The
essence of Hindu and Buddhist teaching lies in the answer to
this. He didn't come out of anywhere and he didn't go anywhere. God must be everywhere if he is anywhere at all. He
is playing hide-and-go-seek *with himself through us*. The part
of himself that forgets he is God, the part that is seeking
himself, is the ego. The part that is hiding is what we call the
unconscious, but it is only hidden or unconscious for as long
as the ego remains *un*conscious of it. Once the ego "wakes

---

[7]That Zen is first and foremost a way of understanding the unconscious is
overlooked by many people. Indeed, as the renowned Zen scholar D.T.
Suzuki writes, "the concept of the unconscious is the foundation of Zen
Buddhism" (*Zen Buddhism: Selected Writings of D.T. Suzuki*, New York:
Anchor Books, 1963, p. 16). One may find it discussed at length in the
teachings of such early Chinese Zen masters as Hui-neng (A.D. 638–713)
and Shen-hui (A.D. 668–770). However, the Zen conception of the unconscious clearly differs from that of Western psychology. As Suzuki comments, "in Zen Buddhism the unconscious is not a psychological term
either in a narrower or in a broader sense . . . . [It is] fundamentally
different from the psychologists' Unconscious. It has a metaphysical con-
notation. When Hui-neng speaks of the Unconscious in Consciousness, he
steps beyond psychology" (*ibid.*, pp. 188, 191). The Unconscious in Zen is,
simply put, the mind of the cosmos. Suzuki on occasion calls it the "Cosmic Unconscious." Yet it is our own unconscious, our higher Self. We are
intimately connected with it. It is beyond us but also within us; as Christ
said, "the kingdom of heaven is within you."

Figure 13. This painting by Salvador Dali is called *Slave Market with Disappearing Bust of Voltaire*. The bust or head of Voltaire is here "disappearing" or hidden because it can only be seen if we bring the sky behind the two cloaked women into the foreground (seeing the sky as the bust's forehead); at the same time, we must push the women's faces, hats, and other apparel into the background (seeing them as the different parts of the face). In other words, figure and ground must be reversed. This play upon perception may be seen as an analogy for how the ego and the unconscious are related. The unconscious (the Gestalt of the bust) is always present, but we can only see it when our egos (the individual figures of the women) are no longer the focus of attention. Of course, in the painting we can, in any given instant, focus on only one scenario *or* the other—we cannot appreciate both simultaneously. In an actual occurrence of *satori* or grace, the dual realities of the ego and the unconscious are experienced simultaneously and single-mindedly. *Slave Market with Disappearing Bust of Voltaire*, 1940. Oil on canvas, 18 ¼ × 25 ¾". Used by permission of the Salvador Dali Museum, St. Petersburg, Florida USA.

up" and becomes conscious of what was formerly unconscious, God has found himself; that is, the ego has discovered that its essential nature was always of God.[8]

The awakening of the ego to its true nature is known in Buddhism as enlightenment; in Zen it is called *satori*. Contrary to what some believe, *satori* is not the dissolution or abolishment of the ego. We need an ego — and a well-developed one — in order to survive. *Satori* is simply the disillusionment or transcendence of the ego's *perspective* of itself as other than the world and the world as other than the Absolute. The Christian counterpart to this, as deducible from Patsy Neal's account, is indeed the "state of grace," a state of mind in which everything is perceived as flowing from God. Theologically, the principle of grace — of God giving his "favor" to humanity — makes possible the incarnation of God's spirit in the world, a process symbolized through the figure of Christ.

The experience of grace or *satori* appears to be the quintessence of mysticism. Because it is an experience of the mind's union or oneness with the world and God, most psychologists do not give much credence to its possibility. Even Jung writes that, "The experience of 'at-one-ment' is one example of those 'quick-knowing' realizations of the East, an intuition of what it would be like if one could exist and not exist at the same time. If I were a Moslem, I should maintain that the power of the All-Compassionate is infinite, and that He alone can make a man to be and not to be at the same time. But for my part I cannot conceive of such a possibility. I therefore assume that in this point, Eastern intuition has

---

[8]To many, this line of thinking may smack of pantheism. However, as a number of scholars have argued, Hinduism and Buddhism are not pantheistic but pan*en*theistic, and in this regard not dissimilar from Judeo-Christianity. Pantheism holds that all is God. Panentheism holds that all is *in* God. The difference is subtle but exists.

overreached itself."⁹ Jung's view is of interest not only because it mirrors psychology and Western thought in general, but because it plays out and plays into the hide-and-go-seek phenomenon insofar as it helps keep God hidden and us seeking for him beyond ourselves. It furthermore shows the points at which the mystical understanding of the unconscious departs from the psychological one. Let us take a closer look at this view.

In Jung's thought, it is evident that the concept of self-realization contrasts sharply with the Eastern concept and with mystical thinking in general. Jung believed that the ego and the unconscious self are distinctly separate entities. Consequently, their relationship cannot feature the experience of oneness that is intrinsic to mysticism. Their relationship is at best a "vis-à-vis," a dualistic encounter or dialogue (as observable for instance in Jung's Philemon dialogues). Thus does Jung also claim that it is "only by indirect means"[10] that we may come to know the unconscious.

These means—dreams, fantasies, visions, etc.—are extremely valuable, yet according to at least Eastern systems, they are not a direct knowledge of the Self but representations or secondary manifestations of it. This applies to their content as well: in Jung's system, the God or self archetype is understood as an *archetype*, but not in terms of the thing-in-itself. Like the philosopher Immanuel Kant by whom he was influenced, Jung did not believe in the possibility of knowing

---

⁹From *The Collected Works of C. G. Jung*, translated by R.F.C. Hull, Bollingen Series XX, Vol. 11, *Psychology and Religion: West and East*, p. 505. Copyright © 1958, 1969 by Princeton University Press. Used by permission.

[10]*Ibid.*, p. 484.

the "thing-in-itself," or as he reconceptualized it, the "archetype-in-itself."[11]

But perhaps most significant of all is that Jung did not believe that the unconscious could possess a dynamic consciousness aside from the quasi-consciousness of the archetypes. This of course means that he did not recognize it as the mind of the cosmos or God. To Jung, the self is not the living Self of God, but the total personality of the collective unconscious or psyche; it may be God*like* but it is not God. Just as the unconscious cannot be perceived directly, so too God cannot be perceived through the unconscious, or any other way, for that matter. Although Jung asserts that the unconscious is "the only available source of religious experience," he is quick to point out that whatever "the further cause of such experience may be, the answer to this lies beyond the range of human knowledge. Knowledge of God is a transcendental problem."[12] By contrast, in mysticism the transcendent may be experienced as immanent.

Given the above framework, one can understand why Jung felt that Eastern intuition overreaches itself when it claims "at-one-ment." However, this attitude is fundamentally no different than Freud's; it is merely the other side of the same coin. To attribute the experience of oneness to the imagination of an ego aspiring to overstep its limits is no different than reducing this experience as the ego's regression to the "oceanic womb feeling" which the fetus supposedly enjoys. Jung sees this experience as beyond the ego;

---

[11]From *The Collected Works of C. G. Jung*, translated by R.F.C. Hull, Bollingen Series XX, Vol. 8, *The Structure and Dynamics of the Psyche*, p. 213. Copyright © 1960, 1969 by Princeton University Press. The English translation renders *"archetype an sich"* as "archetype as such." Jung is in fact alluding to Kant's *"ding an sich,"* i.e., "thing-in-itself" or "thing as such." [12]From *The Collected Works of C. G. Jung*, translated by R.F.C. Hull, Bollingen Series XX, Vol. 10, *Civilization in Transition*, p. 293. Copyright © 1964, 1970 by Princeton University Press. Used by permission.

Freud sees it as occurring before the ego. Neither view is complimentary. However, most unfounded are the suspicions by both psychologists that this experience would be an aberration. If one has a well-developed ego, one will not be "swallowed" by the unconscious or the cosmos. The writings of mystics through the ages amply bear witness to this.

Of course, Jung's view is merely a reflection of the larger tradition from which it arises—namely, Western civilization. The *Weltanschauung* or worldview of Western civilization is rooted in a fundamental schism or split between man and God. As conveyed through the biblical "fall of Adam," man and all of creation with him were "exiled" from the world of God, the "Garden of Eden." The psychological impact of this perceived schism—which is also a schism between the lower self (or ego) and higher Self—has affected the entire course of the Western intellectual tradition. This includes theology, philosophy, and psychology. However, only that part of religion that has been identified as mysticism responds to this schism with any real sense of resolve.

Jewish, Christian, and Islamic mysticism abound with teachings and practices aimed at mending this schism, or rather, overcoming the perception that it exists. This points to why many mystics in the West, unlike the East, were relegated to an underground or taboo status, often excommunicated by the official religious authorities and on occasion even executed. Their views were simply too threatening to the established socioreligious orders. It is not difficult to see why, for example, Pope John XXII—whose responsibility it was to uphold the Church in its role as mediator between a fallen humanity and its God—would find the nondualistic teachings of a mystic like Meister Eckhart heretical. The Church, especially the Church of the Inquisition, was not likely to tolerate someone who went about preaching that, "The eye by which I see God is the same as the eye by which God sees me. My eye and God's eye are one and the same—

one in seeing, one in knowing, and one in loving."[13] Because such ideas were overtly expressed in the foundational scriptures and dogmas of the major Eastern religions, Eastern mystics who wished to proclaim them publicly could do so without fear of being ostracized.

It may be of interest to note that Jung's views on mystical experience may have changed with a later experience. Apparently, this experience occurred too late for him to write about. His earlier experiences, recounted at length in his autobiography, of course are mystical too, but they do not seem to reflect the kind of God-consciousness which, for example, is central to Eckhart. As with Eastern thought, Jung wrote about Eckhart in a way which was too narrowly psychological.[14] However, his views on both may have changed, again, with this final experience. On his deathbed, Jung was reading Charles Luk's *Ch'an and Zen Teachings: First Series*. He expressly asked his colleague, Marie-Louise von Franz, to write Luk a letter describing how he "was enthusiastic. . . . When he read what Hsu Yun said, he sometimes felt as if he himself could have said exactly this! It was just 'it'!"[15]

Whatever insight occurred to ignite Jung's enthusiasm also seemed to evoke a sense of conviction that is absent in his earlier writings on the East. It is probably no accident that this insight occurred while he was dying. Certainly, the process of dying has been known to generate Zenlike insights,

[13]Meister Eckhart, *Meister Eckhart: A Modern Translation*, translated by Raymond B. Blakney (New York: Harper & Row, 1941), p. 206.

[14]See *The Collected Works of C. G. Jung*, translated by R.F.C. Hull, Bollingen Series XX, Vol. 9, II, *Aion: Researches into the Phenomenlogy of the Self*, pp. 193–94.

[15]From an unpublished letter from Marie-Louise von Franz to Charles Luk, dated September 12, 1961; cited by Huston Smith in his Foreword to Philip Kapleau, *The Three Pillars of Zen: Teaching, Practice, and Enlightenment* (New York: Doubleday, a division of Bantam, Doubleday, Dell Publishing Group, Inc., 1980), p. xi.

Figure 14. *Having fallen into a gentle sleep*
Yadwigha, in a dream,
Heard the sounds of a musette
Played by a benevolent magician.
While the moon shone down
Upon the flowers, the green trees,
The wild serpents listened to
The instrument's merry tunes.

Taken from a pamphlet of the
Salon des Indépendents, 1910

The works of Henri Rousseau suggest a quality of *lila*, of the splendor of the world, particularly the animal kingdom. That this scene is a dream invention of Yadwigha's might further suggest that creation is a form of play, perhaps like the tune played by the enchantress. *The Dream*, 1910, oil on canvas, 6' 8 1/2" × 9' 9 1/2". Collection, The Museum of Modern Art, New York. Gift of Nelson A. Rockefeller.

and reversely, Zenlike insights involve a transformation process comparable to dying insofar as the ego's sovereign perspective must be let go of in order for the perspective of the
Self to emerge. As Shakespeare repeatedly demonstrated,
"The King must die." Or, as depicted in Christianity, the
historical Jesus must be crucified in order for him to be resur-
rected as the eternal, cosmic Christ.

🙌

Earlier we defined *lila* as God playing in the world of
forms. When one, for example, goes on a safari in Africa and
is awed by the diverse profusion of life forms—some of
them, like giraffes and zebras, truly comical in appearance—
one is acknowledging *lila*. But as we have discussed, *lila* is
not only God *playing* in the world of forms, it is God *masking
himself* in the world of forms. This is what makes the ego-Self
dichotomy or the game of hide-and-go-seek possible.

Of course, it must be understood that *there is nothing
wrong* with this game: if it is good enough for God to play, it
is good enough for us to accept, to play along. Yet it is also
good for us to know that it *is* a game. For if we truly know
this, then we have found ourselves—our true selves—and
we can play that much better. We can let go to the dramas in
our lives in a way in which we see that *we* are having the
dramas as opposed to *them* having *us*. We don't have to panic
or despair when the going gets rough, for the dramas will
not consume or destroy us, though they may appear to. The
theater of life's events provides us the opportunities to
develop and test our character, to play out life for all that it
has to offer, to live it fully. This would seem afterall to be
God's pleasure: he does not play in order to punish us or the
world; he plays because he likes to. Perhaps Voltaire was
right when he said, "God is a comedian playing to an audi-
ence who is afraid to laugh." Of course, he was here express-
ing one of the more sublime, tragic qualities of *lila*, namely,
the fact that we do not see God in his disguises.

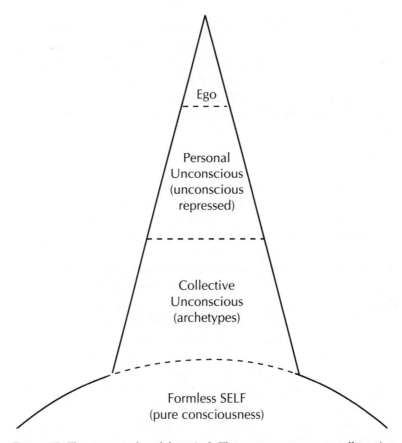

Figure 15. The topography of the mind. The ego represents a small portion of the mind's potential, yet is the seat of our day-to-day functioning. It is the focus of concern of ego psychology, a school of Freud's followers consisting of such thinkers as Anna Freud, Heinz Hartmann, and D. W. Winnicott. Below the ego is the personal unconscious or unconscious repressed, the main focus of Freud. It represents everything that once was conscious (*i.e.*, belonged to the ego), but was either forgotten or repressed. Below this is the collective unconscious with its archetypes; it is shared in common by all humanity and is inherited. It is Jung's main focus. Below the collective unconscious is the Self, a pure consciousness that has no limited form such as that which defines the ego, the personal unconscious, or the archetypes. It is the innermost core of the mind, and is the focus of Hindu and Buddhist thinking. The Christian mystic Meister Eckhart refers to it as God-consciousness. (Adapted from a diagram from Philip Kapleau: *The Three Pillars of Zen*, Beacon Press, 1967. Used by permission.)

I would like to illustrate the principle of *lila* using a couple of illustrations so that we can easily see how the ego and the Self, or the human mind and God's mind, are related. Figure 15 (see page 150) is based on a schema of the Buddhist conception of this, though it is similar to the Hindu (especially Vedantist) conception as well. The schema was originally developed by the modern Zen master Sogaku Harada.[16] I have modified it to suit our purposes, but its basic features remain unchanged.

In fig. 15, we see the basic topography of the psyche as it was laid out in chapter 2. What is different here is the overall context of this topography and the added layer or dimension of the Self beneath the collective unconscious. I shall speak of the overall context first.

The psyche is here compared to "a wave on the vast ocean; its brief existence seems apart from the ocean—and in a sense it is not the ocean—but in *substance* it is not other than the ocean, out of which it arose, into which it will recede, and from which it will emerge again as a new wave. In just the same way, individual consciousness issues from pure consciousness and in its essential nature is indistinguishable from it. Their common element, the viable Void, is shown in the diagram by the all-pervading white background."[17] This "all-pervading white background" is itself the overall context in which the psyche is to be seen. Stated simply, it is the universe, here called the Void for a certain empty quality it has: when the universe is perceived as a single, infinite expanse with nothing separate in it or beside it to quantify it or contrast it to, it has the sensation of being nothing at all and is hence experienced as a Void. It is "viable," however, because it is not mere nothingness but full of all the possibilities of existence. The Kabbalists describe God also as the absolute "Nothing," and Meister Eckhart's descriptions lean in this direction as well.

---

[16]The original diagram is presented with a commentary by Philip Kapleau in Philip Kapleau, *op. cit.*, p. 328.
[17]*Ibid*.

The wave-ocean analogy of the schema explains not only how the many arise from the One but how the One inhabits the many. The substance of water is immanent in both the wave and the ocean. From the viewpoint of the surface of the ocean, from the individualistic, egoistic wave-forms, the world is multiplistic. There are many waves, many egos. All seem separate and unique. But from the viewpoint of the transcendent, foundation level of the ocean, where all is one, the oft-stormy turmoil of the fragmented waves above does not exist. Yet the oneness characteristic of the foundation level exists not only "down there"; it pervades all the levels and opens up into and as the all-pervading white background of everything. Thus, as was mentioned also in regard to Jung's psychoid layer, its metaphorical topography should not be taken literally.

Speaking of Jung's psychoid layer, we may find certain similarities between it and the Buddhist concept of the Self. If we recall our discussion of the former, it too is transcendent and pervades all of reality. Yet it is not the Self for it is not envisioned as pure consciousness or as perceptible by the human mind. Or, if the psychoid layer is the Self, it is so with these attributes, contrary to Jung's formulations. In any event, we can see how Jung's formulations of the self also differed: he did not see it as a level of pure consciousness *beyond* the collective unconscious. Because he believed that the collective unconscious was the final level that the mind could perceive, he had to settle for an indirect encounter with the Self as it is perceptually *filtered through* the collective unconscious.

This filtering process is what in Jung's psychology gives the Self its archetypal qualities, such as symbols and images. What one in fact experiences are, again, the manifestations of the Self, but not the Self-in-itself. In Buddhism, the collective unconscious may be by-passed, so to speak, for a direct experience of the Self. We may say that Buddhism approaches the unconscious as a field of pure consciousness or intelligence, whereas Jung approaches it as a field of contents, personal as well as collective. Actually, as we see, Buddhism integrates both fields into a single schema. In Harada's original model, the collective unconscious is referred to as the *"alaya-vijnana,"* a Tibetan Buddhist concept which most closely parallels the collective unconscious.[18]

Figure 16 (page 154) views the somewhat impersonal schema we have just discussed from a particularly "human" angle. It was devised by the philosopher Huston Smith, and is based on his studies of the ancient teachings of the world's religions.[19] It shows how the human being is related to different levels of reality. Each ring of the circle represents a different level or sphere. The terrestrial level, which the body is on, is the physical realm. The term "mind" may here correspond to "ego," "soul" to "psyche" (which would include the collective unconscious), and "spirit" to "Self." Like the formless Self, the spirit and the infinite open up to an all-pervading white background. That the soul is "celestial" goes to say that it is the realm of the archetypal "angels" or forces. It may also be connected with the realm of the afterlife and other realms which we know little about.

ℐ⁂

There is a wonderful parable of somebody who knocks on the door of God's private chamber.[20] God says, "Who's there?" The person responds, "It is I." God says, "Go away." The person goes away. Some time later he returns, and knocks again. God asks, "Who's there?" The person says, "It is Thou." God replies, "Come in." Of course, one cannot

---

[18]See Lama Anagarika Govinda, *Foundations of Tibetan Mysticism* (York Beach, ME: Samuel Weiser, Inc., 1970; and London: Rider & Co., 1970), pp. 73, 83. See also Alan Watts, *In My Own Way: An Autobiography* (New York: Vintage Books, Random House, 1973), pp. 391–92.

[19]Huston Smith, *Forgotten Truth: The Primordial Tradition* (New York: Harper & Row, 1976), p. 62.

[20]Cited in Joko Beck, *Everyday Zen* (New York: HarperCollins, 1989).

artificially induce an awareness that one is God. However, the attempt to nurture in the course of our daily schedules some moments of awareness of our higher nature is central to almost all traditions of meditation and prayer. Such

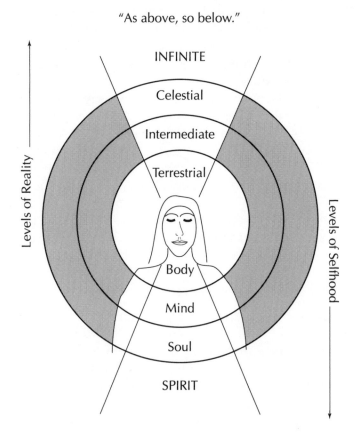

"As above, so below."

INFINITE

Celestial

Intermediate

Terrestrial

Body

Mind

Soul

SPIRIT

Levels of Reality

Levels of Selfhood

Figure 16. This diagram incorporates the physical, psychological, and metaphysical realms into a single schema. By correlating different levels of selfhood with different levels of reality, it illustrates how the intrapsychic is connected to the suprapsychic, and how, in fact, the two may be indistinguishable from each other. (Diagram based on a drawing from *Forgotten Truth*, by Huston Smith. Copyright © 1976 by Huston Smith. Used by permission of Harper & Row, Publishers, Inc.)

moments have a way of reproducing themselves and sprouting up here and there in the midst of the day's activities, filtering their benefits into them. Eventually, as this continues, a new center in our consciousness may emerge and we may experience a "place" within ourselves from which we can watch our dramas unfold with greater clarity and a sense of spiritual peace.

This newly emergent center of consciousness is known in various traditions as the "witness" or the "observing self." If not the Self, it is a sort of vestibule to it. When we get angry, it may ask us, "But *who* is it who is angry?" When we are depressed, it inquires, "*What* is depressed?" Soon we see that most of our states of mind are precisely that: states of mind. They pass. As we identify less with them and easier let them go, we see that what remains constant and steady in our minds is our perpetual witness, an underlying consciousness that is pure and independent of our moods, feelings, and thoughts. It watches everything that occurs in a detached yet at the same time all-embracing, compassionate manner. Whether the moments during which we tune into the witness are the results of meditation, prayer, or some other meditative activity, they may become little oases or retreats of contemplation throughout our otherwise hectic day. And as they increase and spill over more and more into our activities, slowly this new center of awareness grows closer to our ego, or perhaps vice versa, our ego grows into it. In this way do the ego and the Self find common ground in the real world of our day-to-day experiences; in this way does the ego enter the chamber of the Lord.

It would seem that the aim of human growth—on both individual and collective levels—is to attain a realization of the deeper levels of Selfhood. It would appear that the purpose of life—if there is such a thing—is for us to become God, who is in fact whom we essentially are. Discovering our essential nature seems central to understanding who we are and what we are in this world. Of course, I do not speak here so much of a particular experience of realization, such as an experience of *satori* or grace. As Abraham Maslow has indicated, such experiences are "peak-experiences." Though the acme of religious encounter, they are often but glimpses, fleeting moments of expanded awareness. They too pass. It is the spiritual understanding and wisdom that endure, and thus, Self-realization is not to be thought of as a climactic goal, but an ongoing process.

Why we must undergo such an apparently evolutionary process to become what we already and always were is a puzzle to which there is no easy answer. Pierre Teilhard de Chardin suggests this process is necessary for a "converging universe."[21] This is a universe moving toward its pre-existing, transcendent "center of unification" (God), a universe in which humanity is in a state of becoming as opposed to a state of being static. Perhaps this is but a Western scientist's version of the ancient Hindu idea of *lila*, of the Godhead playing hide-and-go-seek with itself through everything, including us and perhaps especially us. In any event, paradoxical as it may seem, the becoming or unfolding of our realization is not a challenge of attaining something that is "not yet"; it is a challenge of realizing something that "already is." The Zen masters whisper to us: "One in all, All in one—if only this is realized, no more worry about not being perfect."

---

[21]Pierre Teilhard de Chardin, *The Phenomenon of Man* (New York: Harper & Row, 1965).

CHAPTER 6

THE TWILIGHT ZONE

Most of the people I see in my psychotherapy practice suffer from what the psychiatrist Harry Stack Sullivan called difficulties in living—depression, anxiety, stress, loneliness, marital discord or other relationship conflicts, inability to cope with life transitions, and so forth. As these are problems of everyday existence, they are by no means uncommon and very much represent the "stuff of life." However, every once in a while clients will recount experiences which are not quite ordinary. Their "stuff" seems to come, at least at first glance, from some place other than everyday life. We'll discuss two such experiences, and although they are only two examples, there are many like them.[1]

✿

Victor T. began therapy to explore his confusion around vocational issues, though clearly these issues involved more than the usual kind of career decisions. He was 23, had planned to enter the priesthood for a number of years, and was studying theology at a Jesuit university in preparation. However, not too long before coming to see me, he had

---

[1]Victor T. and Ellen S. are fictitious names used to protect the identities of clients who have given permission to use their cases.

become romantically involved with a young woman. Largely in response to this he had changed his mind and decided not to become a priest. He felt comfortable with this decision for a while, but soon all kinds of doubts began to creep in. He could not sort out whether or not he had a genuine "calling" to the priesthood. He emotionally withdrew from his girlfriend, though continued to see her platonically. His confusion around whether he should indeed become a priest and whether he should continue to see this girl prompted him to start therapy; he felt he needed the professional assistance of someone not affiliated with the clergy.

After a couple months of therapy, Victor began one session by telling me about an unusual experience. It had happened earlier that week and involved his girlfriend—or rather, his friend—Denise. I asked him at the end of the session to give me a written account of the experience, and he wrote the following:

On Tuesday evening Denise and I went to a restaurant. Around 11:00, I was driving her home. Her neighborhood is quite residential and quiet at night, with very little traffic on the streets. The streets are also very dark at night.

About a mile from Denise's house we turned off a main boulevard. It was so dark I had to put on the high beams. Suddenly I had a strange and strong feeling that we were being followed. I looked in the mirror: darkness was all I could see. The intensity of the feeling grew, and I became uneasy. I braked until we came to a stop, and I turned in my seat to directly scan the long street behind us. I saw no movement. Denise asked me what was the matter, and I told her. She laughed and asked if it was the Maltese falcon they were after. I told her I was not joking, that I had never had this kind of feeling before.

We drove on. The feeling persisted and intensified. Again I braked and scanned behind us. I saw nothing. Denise laughed again, insisting that I was trying to put one over on her. I continued to drive, until I finally felt compelled to stop the car and actually get out and look behind. I could see nothing, I could hear nothing. Resuming the drive, it suddenly dawned on me that whoever was following us was above us and not behind us. Again I stopped the car and got out. The sky was clear except for a couple of clouds, there was no moon, and the stars were brightly lit. Denise was now having a good laugh, convinced that I was playing a prank. I had once played a prank on her, and so it was not surprising that she was expecting another. Nevertheless, I insisted that this was no prank.

I drove on. Suddenly, in front of the car and to the right, on somebody's lawn, a white light in the shape of a circle about two feet in diameter, "opened" and "closed" within a moment's passing. I slammed on the brakes. I knew this could not have come from my car because the beam from the car light was sharply delineated from the surrounding darkness in which I saw the circular light. Excitedly I asked Denise, "Did you see that!?" Laughing, she said, "See what?" I got out of the car again and searched the sky. Denise, still sitting in the car, hummed the theme from the TV show *The Twilight Zone*. I felt her mockery at this point was beyond what was called for, as I had never been much of a sky-watcher nor had I ever had a UFO experience or expressed any desire to have one.

Driving on, I saw in front of the car, to the left this time, two globes of light appear and just as quickly disappear. One was on a lawn, the other on the wall of a house. The one on the lawn seemed bigger. Later, as I recalled their appearance, it occurred to me that there were no beams attached to them. Seeing them, I again abruptly brought the car to a halt and shouted to Denise, "Now that! Did you see that!?" "See what?," she responded in a dead-pan manner. Annoyed, I asked her if she was blind. I got out of the car and spent five minutes examining the sky, but as before I could see nothing unusual.

Finally we turned off the street to another street which would take us to Denise's house. I made a U-turn in front of her house, parked the car and turned off the engine. Smiling and obviously in good humor, Denise said, "You know, you really are crazy." As I looked at her, I saw in the upper right corner of the windshield a reddish light moving at about helicopter height. It was darting about in an erratic manner which I immediately knew could not belong to a manmade object. I said to Denise, "I'm not crazy. Look over there." Denise looked. I could sense her entire demeanor change as she asked with alarm, "What is it?" "I don't know," I said. "But whatever it is, it's following us."

We got out of the car. We stood watching for a minute, and Denise again asked what it was. I shrugged my shoulders, as I was myself trying to figure out what it was. The reddish light looked like an electric light. The "object" was too far for its shape to be made out apart from the light; it looked as if the light pretty much encompassed the object. When seen at a certain moment against the background of a small cloud, there could be no doubt that it was within the earth's atmosphere. To our eyes it looked like one quarter the size of a dime, which means that if it was one half to one mile away from us, it could have been quite a large object.

The object's movements were especially peculiar. It moved in short bursts of straight lines which were then followed by movements in directions which were often acute angles to the former lines. The object looked as if it were making triangles and trapeziums. Its movements looked like this:

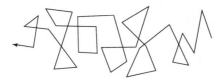

The movements were extremely fast, yet before each directional change, the object seemed to stop for a moment. There was apparently no logical, fixed pattern to the specific movements, but it became evident after five or six minutes that the object was moving across the sky in a large arc, and that we seemed to be the center point around which it moved. It arced from our southwestern view of the sky right over to our eastern view. As it reached the latter, it seemed closer to us. At this point, it stopped traveling in its arc, otherwise it would have started to move farther away from us. Here, it just stayed localized, but continued its erratic, angular movements. I would say eight or nine minutes had passed since our original sighting of it until it reached this position in the sky.

During all this, not a single sound could be heard coming from the object's direction. From its movements, I could only conclude that the object was not a helicopter, an airplane, a satellite, a weather balloon, or a meteor or falling star. I had never seen anything like it.

Denise became frightened as it became evident that the object was moving closer to us and that we seemed to be the center point around which it moved. For myself, I also felt nervous, but mostly I felt curious. Whatever the object was, I knew that I had sensed its presence before it appeared and that it was responsible for the globes of light which I saw. I suspected that I was having some kind of communication with it.

As the object angulated in its localized position above us, I wondered what would happen next. Suddenly an "urge" or forceful thought came to me much like the earlier feeling that we were being followed. There was an empty, grassy field beside Denise's house. The urge "told me" to go into the field. I thought about it for a few moments. "Denise," I said, "I'm going into the field. Wait here." Denise took hold of my arm and began pleading with me not to go. I told her to calm down and not to worry. She asked me what I was going to do in the field. I told her I didn't know, I would just sit down and wait and see what would happen. My impression was that I would just close my eyes and empty my mind; perhaps a communication would come through. Denise was afraid of something else: "Look, they may come down and take you into that ship. They may take you away and you'd never come back."

Denise's point had crossed my mind. We were dealing with something absolutely unknown. I quickly thought things over again, and came to my original conclusion: it was a risk worth taking in order to encounter something as novel as this. But moreover, I think I had sensed that that "ship" bode no ill will. If they had wanted to harm or "capture" me, they could already have done so. "Denise," I said, "I'll take a chance." At this moment she became panicky. She began to cry, her voice trembled, and she was clutching my arm in an uncomfortably tight grip. We argued for a minute, until I realized there was no point. I couldn't leave her. I wasn't even in the field yet and she was already nearly having an anxiety attack.

I cleared my mind and tried to send out a "message." I thought, "Now is not the right time. Perhaps another time." Immediately I intuitively "felt" a response: "Okay." Suddenly, the object dashed downward at a very high speed and disappeared "into" the sky. It was as if an invisible zipper had opened the sky and then closed it after the object vanished into the opening. And thus ended this strange event.

⁂

Jung speculated as early as 1958 that UFO phenomena may be unconscious manifestations—particularly, manifestations of the self archetype. He postulated that because we are out-of-touch with the unconscious, with the inner self, it manifests in an extreme yet enticing way, compelling us to recognize it. In days of old, similar archetypal manifestations would occur through forms that were culturally viable options for those times: angels, fairies, elves, leprechauns, mermaids, trolls, lutins, fawns, etc. (We might add to this array such elusive, nocturnal creatures as the big foot and the Loch Ness monster, sightings of which have also been reported through the centuries.) Jung argued that such phenomena were basically projections of the psyche.

Since 1958, UFO reports have increased. They include not only sightings, but dramatic abductions by extraterrestrial beings. Ultimately, we cannot rule out the possibility and even likelihood of life on other planets: this is a huge universe. However, the fact that many UFO accounts reveal some involvement of the unconscious (e.g., many encounters occur in a hypnagogic, dreamlike state) suggests that Jung's theory may have an authentic basis. As one alleged abductee, Whitley Strieber, writes, "Whomever or whatever the visitors are . . . [they] are involved with us on very deep levels, playing in the band of dream, weaving imagination and reality together until they begin to seem what they probably are—aspects of a single continuum. . . . I cannot say, in all truth, that I am certain the visitors are present as entities entirely independent of their observers. Nor can I say that I do not think they are here at all."[2] This statement points to

---

[2]Whitley Strieber, *Communion: A True Story* (New York: Avon Books, 1988), pp. 246, 294.

Figure 17. This drawing is one among many which the artist calls his "Angel Series." His concept of angels as phenomena of the unconscious is devoid of traditional, anthropomorphic images. That these angels are, however, the same heavenly beings the ancients referred to is indicated by the winged formations descending from the sky. Especially interesting is the similarity of structure in these formations with the structure of the rooftops, implying that what we project into the sky as our archetypes are essentially the same as what we project onto the earth as our architecture: both are born out of the creative imagination. Perhaps UFOs, the modern versions of angels, are a kind of psychic architecture. Ira Stein, *Angels*, New York, 1990. Used by permission.

the distinct possibility that the "visitors" may be autono-mous complexes of the collective unconscious, which, as we discussed earlier, indeed appears to be a single continuum with multiple dimensions.

The question this raises is: how can UFOs be manifesta-tions of the unconscious if they exist in the physical dimen-sion? Of course, having set forth that the unconscious is a single continuum, it is understandable that it could *extend* itself into the physical. We have observed such extension in the synchronicities, precognitions, and visions we have read about. But extension into the physical is a far cry from mate-rialization *as* the physical. Can the unconscious actually cause objects to appear and disappear as if they were materi-alizing and dematerializing into thin air? Was the UFO that Victor and Denise saw "real?" If a projection, did it consist of matter? The large body of UFO literature certainly treats UFO phenomena as materially real. It cites numerous instances of UFOs that have been registered on radar and have left high-temperature burns and high-pressure imprints in the ground as well as radioactive traces on cars and people's bodies. If the unconscious is responsible for these events, it tells us a great deal not only about UFO phenomena, but about the capacities and power of the unconscious mind.

Of course, nobody has any real closure on this matter, and nobody has scientifically demonstrated that the uncon-scious can materialize and dematerialize objects. Usually such phenomena occur unexpectedly and in anything but ideal laboratory conditions. Nevertheless, experiences involving the materialization and dematerialization of objects do occur, and some of them are more explicit than UFO experiences. Before continuing with our discussion on UFOs, let's look at an account written by another client, Ellen S. It is about a childhood experience which addresses the possibility of such materialization and dematerialization. Since the discussion of this experience came up well into the course of treatment and is not overtly related to the issues for which Ellen came for therapy, I will not offer background information but proceed directly with her account:

My parents are survivors of the Holocaust, and when I was 7, a very dear friend of theirs, who had endured with them the tyranny of a labor camp, was coming to see them for the first time since the war ended. He was coming from Vienna, and I had never met him before. As I understood it, he was going to stay at the home of a relative and visit us on alternate days.

The day this gentleman made his first appearance at our home, he presented my sister and me with generous gifts. To my sister, who was 4 at the time, he gave a gold chain necklace attached to a gold-plated American penny. To me he gave a similar gold chain, but attached to it was a Star of David—the ancient symbol of the Jewish people and religion. I had already begun my formal religious education in Jewish Sunday school, and, adding what my parents had taught me, I had strong emotional associations to this gift. Receiving it was the equivalent of a Christian child receiving a Cross: it meant "God." Also, it was imbued with nuances I had absorbed from the many colorful biblical stories I was learning in religious school. Some of these stories of course included King David and such impressive scenarios as his going up against the giant Goliath.

So, needless to say, I was quite pleased with my gift. My mother took my sister and me aside and, fearing we might lose or misplace these gifts, warned us that they were very valuable and we should not take them off our necks. Naturally, we agreed.

Two nights later, the following event occurred. I was in my room, preparing to go to bed. I wanted to see the Star close up, as I was weary of looking at it from a distance while facing a mirror—which was the only way I could see it because the chain did not hang low enough on my neck for the Star to be in my field of vision. My impulsiveness getting the better of me, I could not resist: I disobeyed my mother and took the chain off my neck. I was holding it in my hand while I was sitting on my bed. Nobody was in the room. I was enjoying looking at this beautiful piece of jewelry, the most precious thing that had ever been given to me. Suddenly, somehow, it slipped out of my hand. I saw it fall down along the side of the bed and heard it hit the floor. I immediately looked over to see where it fell, and saw it coiled up on the leaf of a flower which was part of the pattern on the linoleum floor of my room. I took my eyes off it only for a moment, long enough for me to get off the bed and get it. As I bent down to pick it up, it was gone. Absolutely gone. Nowhere to be seen. I was certain I had not been clumsy and accidentally kicked the chain, but just in case, I started looking all over the floor around and underneath the bed. I looked with my eyes, and I looked with my hands. As my panic grew, I started to search the entire floor of the room. I even moved the bed to the other side of the room, and inch by inch inspected the side where the bed had originally been.

At this point, my mother made her timely entrance. "What's going on in here?," she asked. I knew I was in trouble. I told her the truth. She looked at me with disdain, and then glanced about the floor. She walked around the room once, but saw nothing. She then looked at me again and said, "Go to bed. We'll look for it tomorrow."

The next day witnessed a complete overhaul of my room. My mother and I went through it with a fine-toothed comb. She came in after breakfast (it was a holiday, I had no school), and we stripped the bed of its blankets and sheets, searching everywhere. She then vacuumed the entire floor — also moving the bed from one side of the room to the other — and emptied the vacuum cleaner bag to see if the chain and Star were in it. But no luck. My mother was as baffled as I:

this was not such a small piece of jewelry that it could escape both the eye and a thorough vacuuming of the floor. It seemed to have vanished into thin air. My mother expressed grave disappointment in me, and said that if her friend, who would be visiting us again the next day, were to ask why I wasn't wearing the Star of David, I would be obliged to tell him the truth. I felt terrible.

That night, before I went to bed, I again conducted a search of my room, but in vain. Once in bed, my feelings of loss and shame overwhelmed me, and I cried. Then there occurred what I believe is an important element in the story. Throughout my childhood, I was taught, like many children, to pray to God every night before going to bed. I would thank God for all the good things in my life, and pray for health and happiness for my family and myself. My parents were never forceful or dogmatic in these matters, and prayer was taught to me in an inviting way. Moreover, it was presented as a real communication from me to God, with God listening. He may not answer my prayers, but he listens. My sense of prayer thus had, as Martin Buber would say, a genuine I-Thou quality: it was heartfelt and personal, even if childish.

On this night, I prayed for something which was not the usual, and I prayed with real earnestness and passion, with tears. I prayed to God to give me back my Star of David. This is not to say that I blamed God for taking it away, for I had no idea how it disappeared. Simply, I believed that he alone could return it.

The next morning I awoke to the sound of my mother's voice calling my sister and me to get ready for breakfast. My parents' friend was coming and we should hurry. As I got out of bed, my eyes fell upon an unexpected sight. Exactly where two nights before I had dropped the chain and Star—on the leaf of a flower—was lying the same chain and Star, coiled up the same way. Astounded, I brought the pendant to my mother to show her. She also responded with great surprise, especially when she learned where I found it. Over the years we have discussed this incident a number of times. She is still as stricken with its oddness as I am.

Of course, the idea may suggest itself that my mother might have bought and, while I was sleeping, placed a new Star of David on the leaf of the flower—a sort of "tooth fairy" trick. Certainly, there were a number of good reasons why she might have done this. However, I think this explanation can be categorically ruled out. She would long ago have owned up to such a trick, and as I mentioned, her curiosity about this incident is still as genuine as at the time it happened. Also, I should add that the location of the chain and Star upon the leaf of the flower and the way the chain was coiled the morning I found the piece were precisely identical to the location and manner of coiling when I had last seen it two nights earlier. My mother could hardly have duplicated this arrangement, as she was not in the room when I lost the piece and I did not describe to her the specific details of this arrangement. Furthermore, none of this explains how the piece originally disappeared. To me, I must admit, the whole incident was a sort of miracle.

૭

"Miracles" such as Ellen's are difficult to accept, and there is a tendency to dismiss them as aberrations of perception rather than acknowledge them as occurrences in the real world. Cognitive psychologists, for example, can proffer a number of theories to explain such incidents. One such theory holds that perception can become skewed if it becomes too focused or intense. This can produce the opposite effect we desire. For instance, if we are looking too hard for something, we may not notice it even if it is in our field of vision. Indeed, how many times has this happened when we are looking all about for the salt shaker or our keys and they are right there in front of our eyes? Is it possible that this is how Ellen "lost" her Star of David? Not likely. Her visual perception may have been skewed, but how can we explain how this piece of jewelry escaped the touch of her hand, her mother's visual perception, and the suction of a vacuum cleaner? These factors suggest that the piece was simply not there to be found.

It seems that the most viable explanation is that the unconscious either enveloped the Star of David into a non-physical dimension or somehow veiled it or changed it within the physical one in a way that made it undetectable and unobtainable. And of course, it then returned, unveiled, or "reconstituted" it at the opportune moment. To also imply, as indeed Ellen did, that God was responsible for all this should not be too hard to digest at this point in our discussion, for it has already been suggested that the unconscious mind and God are in essence one. Thus, in claiming that it was the mind that performed this "miracle," I would emphasize that it was not *just* the mind that performed it; rather, it was *not less* than the mind that performed it. For if prayer is a power of the mind, it reaches into the unconscious. For this reason has prayer played such a strong role in Western mysticism.

As for why God would perform such a miracle for a child when the world is in need of far greater ones, what can we say? Religious literature is full of similar accounts. Perhaps if as adults we would bring to our problems a similar humility, faith, and passion, our prayers would also be answered. Perhaps in having lost our childlike innocence, we have grown cynical. As the actress Lily Tomlin remarked, "Why is it that when we talk to God, they say we're praying, but when God talks to us, they say we're crazy?"

❧

Let us return to our discussion of UFOs. Even if experiences like Ellen's do suggest that the unconscious can materialize objects, there is no way to ascertain whether the object that Victor and Denise saw, as one example of a UFO sighting, was such a materialization. It could simply have been a vision, one to which both of them were privy. This is not impossible: afterall, the collective unconscious *is* collective. Yet at the same time, as we discussed earlier, it and its visions could be very selective and subjective. In a course I periodically teach on the unconscious, a student once told me of an incident in which she saw a UFO land in a large field behind her house. She called her mother and father over to the window. Curiously, only the father could see the UFO; the mother could not see it. When I questioned the student, she acknowledged that her father had always been open-minded about such matters whereas her mother was skeptical. Evidently, our mental attitude seems to be a vital constituting factor of what we see as "reality." The question here is: whose "vision" was more real?

As Jung said, UFOs may only be projections. However, it is important to keep in mind that they would be projections of the *collective* psyche as opposed to the individual psyche. *We* are in the unconscious as equally as it is in us, and therefore to say that UFOs emanate from the unconscious is to say that they emanate from nature itself. They are spontaneous creations or dreams, so to speak, of the collective unconscious. They are as real as anything else in nature, though like other paranormal phenomena, the principles by which they manifest and operate are not understood. Perhaps UFOs, too, belong to that sublime sphere labeled as celestial in Huston Smith's diagram (see fig. 16 on page 154).

It is in view of this celestial quality that UFOs may be seen as modern angels or messengers, as Jung argues. And if they are indeed materializing and abducting us, the argument would go that we are, in our modern technological world, so oblivious to our inner dream world that its messengers have to literally kidnap us to get their messages across. This seems to be Whitley Strieber's position as well, for as he indicates, the UFO beings who "abducted" him had

Figure 18. What we don't let in the front door breaks in through the back door. Here, a UFO suddenly shatters our conceptions of the world. Its human eye suggests that although it is an unidentified flying object, it is more human than extraterrestrial. Perhaps what is invading us here is a perspective or way of looking at things which is essentially human but has become so "alien" to us that it now has to appear in shocking and unusual forms to attract our attention. Perhaps this is the eye of our own unconscious. Tsuneo Sanda, *Disturbance of Privacy*, Tokyo, 1986. Used by permission.

above all a spiritual message to impart. It seems that, given our concrete, materialistic orientation, we only pay attention to the spiritual when we are physically slapped in the face with it. UFO phenomena have in this regard a special capacity for "disorienting" our orientation: in any single instance they can be explained in a variety of ways, thus lending weight to the impression that they are almost purposely designed with the intent to confound our conscious, logical, scientific faculties. Indeed, this appears to be the lure of UFO phenomena: they seem so real, but never quite real enough for us to walk away with any hard evidence that they exist. As soon as we approach or are about to get some closure, they disappear. While some people see them without a doubt, others don't. They're never quite in this reality, but they're not purely in the mind either. I think Denise was right: they *are* from the Twilight Zone.[3]

꙰

Why do UFOs appear to some people and not others? There is no clear answer. They seem to be spontaneous acts of the collective unconscious, and whoever is there to wit-

---

[3]A word about abduction experiences as an accentuated from of UFO experiences may be in order here since they seem to be occurring more frequently and have a definite "twilight zone" quality. It would appear that such experiences reflect the truism that what we don't let in the front door breaks in through the back door. The more severely we repress or disavow what is within us, the more extreme are the measures the unconscious will take to catch our attention. It seems as if the *unconscious* needs us to recognize it as much as *we* need to recognize it. However, abduction experiences raise a number of concerns. The question of their material objectivity here aside, they strike me as a rather painful way to attain spiritual insight. Contrary to mere sightings and communications, abductions tend to be colored by physical terror as well as psychological violence. UFO beings are consistently reported to perform medical experiments on their subjects, experiments which sound awfully frightening. If these experiences genuinely emanate from the unconscious, they may be likened to seizures or explosive, volcanic eruptions. Such terror is not unheard of in connection to religious experience. As Rudolf Otto shows in *The Idea of the Holy* (translated by John W. Harvey, London: Oxford University Press, 1950), the feeling of terror that may occur as we face the

ness them, is there. This is what can be concluded from the literature and from people who have seen them. However, UFO visitations do not always have to be initiated only by the inhabitants of the celestial world; they may be mutually initiated by both them and us. If we examine the experience of Victor and Denise in a psychological light, we see that it may have been an example of this. Allow me to explain.

When clients report a religious experience, I will often ask them to contemplate the *context* in which it occurred. This may be very revealing, for the experience may have as much of a bearing upon their personal world of time, space, and private emotions as on the transcendent world of God or the unconscious. In fact, often such experiences come from the transcendent world or the unconscious with messages to convey about our world of time, space, and emotional events. In such an instance, I will ask clients to review the experience in the same way that they might a dream, to see it as a manifestation of the unconscious that may have hidden implications. This is not to deny or minimalize the possibility, for example, that a UFO sighting consists of an objective materialization, but rather to evaluate the sighting from an inner point of view and perhaps ascertain its deeper, subjective significance. What unconscious pattern of behavior is being "sighted" or "seen" besides the UFO? What is the "unidentified flying object" a symbol of, as it were?

---

[3](cont.) *mysterium tremendum* is a very prominent feature in the history of religion. And of course, there is the dark, terrible side of God—the not good hand—which we read about in the literatures of almost all the world religions. The Old and New Testaments abound with references to God's wrath. However, it is predominantly God's love and good will that are universally lauded. In a similar spirit, religious experience as recorded through the ages draws its strength from the deep joy and sense of well-being it promotes. As can be gathered from dozens of accounts like Strieber's, abduction experiences lack these qualities. Whatever they are, one wonders if they genuinely belong to that order of experience we call religious. For the still good hand of God is not only still good. It is still *and* good. It is the same hand that leads us beside still waters and restores our souls. Such are not the waters to which UFO abductions lead.

In Victor's instance, it is curious that his UFO encounter came in the midst of a painful dilemma or struggle to decide whether he should become a priest. He came from a devout Catholic family with a long, cherished tradition of producing priests and nuns, and it was clear that with him, the youngest child in his generation, this tradition was at risk of being broken; his siblings and cousins had married or pursued other professions. There were thus strong family expectations for him to become a priest. Also noteworthy was how Victor was occupying himself during the period in which his sighting occurred. As the dilemma around his vocation and relationship became more intense, he seemed to increasingly withdraw socially and emotionally. It was summer break and he was not taking any courses at school, yet he would return home from his summer job and spend his evenings studying theology. His studiousness and reclusion seemed to me to be as much a diversion from his problems as a genuine passion for theology.

On the night when the sighting occurred, Denise had pressured Victor, against his will, to go out. He described her to me as a rather gregarious person with down-to-earth qualities. Although Victor admired her for these qualities, he also complained that she was not very spiritual. He claimed that she was an agnostic who didn't understand his spiritual aspirations, who on occasion made fun of him for believing that God would bestow upon him a calling to become a priest and remain celibate for the rest of his life. The term Victor said she used when she teased him is most curious: she would describe him as "too otherworldly."

It is not impossible that the UFO experience Victor and Denise had that night came in response to their psychological situation, a situation in which each represented opposite but complementary tendencies. It is presumptuous to assume that the UFO appeared solely for Victor's benefit even though he was the one who had the premonition and saw the globes of light. The experience as a whole fit the structure of a mutually shared Gestalt. Denise was generally skeptical and cynical of Victor's religious stance. On the night in question, she made fun of his premonition and perception of the globes, but of course, when the object appeared in the sky, her skepticism shattered. As Victor pointed out, if this experience did not imbue Denise with a natural interest in things otherworldly, it certainly did compel her to at least intellectually acknowledge their existence. This experience seemed to come as a compensation for her—shall we say?—earthbound attitude.

For Victor, the compensation was precisely *toward* this attitude: he needed some good binding to Mother Earth. It was clear that the flying object from the celestial sphere represented his own ethereal, theocentric orientation. At the time, his identity was being overextended in this orientation, resulting in a social and emotional withdrawal. Hence the visitation from unidentified aliens—extremely otherworldly. And the choices also reflected the overall structure of the situation: he could risk going into the skies with the sky-gods, or he could stay with Denise on a familiar but level ground. Her emotional appeal was what hooked him to his own "earthy" emotions (what some call the "feminine side"). His "emotional rescue" of her was also, and perhaps mostly, his own self-rescue. As Denise was compensated in her attitude, so was Victor in his; through the UFO encounter, each balanced the other out. It would seem that the unconscious set it up this way.

It is interesting that in Victor's case the UFO incident seemed to represent not his being *out*-of-touch with his inner self, but his being too *in*-touch with it, if such a thing is possible. Too much of something good can be as harmful as not enough, and the unconscious is as likely to comment on one scenario as the other.[4] When I asked Victor to explore the incident in the context of his life and as if it were a dream or

---

[4] I am here reminded of the biblical adage about people who gain the world and lose their souls. Perhaps the other extreme is also possible, and we can gain our souls but lose the world.

message from the unconscious (except one occurring externally), he was able to see how it symbolically paralleled his inner dilemma. As he began to see his predominating orientation as "alien" and "alienating" to his other and more worldly aspirations, he was slowly able to acknowledge that he did not really want to be a priest. He only thought he wanted to be a priest or felt he should be a priest. Of course, this incident was hardly the decisive factor in Victor's final choices, but it did add a colorful element. In the end, realizing that there are many ways to serve God, Victor chose to pursue a career in academic theology, and also began to see Denise again in a romantic way.

It is noteworthy that the theme of encountering UFOs occasionally appears in clients' dreams, and the accompanying dramas are not unlike the one that unfolded in the "real" world with Victor and Denise. I have found that with certain clients presenting certain dreams *or* real-life situations, it is helpful to use an approach which temporarily suspends the distinction between inner and outer worlds and views both as co-equal dimensions of the unconscious. Ultimately, it does not make a difference whether the UFO Victor and Denise saw was materially real. Its *meaning* was real. Likewise, a dream may be absurd or bizarre when viewed in terms of the real world, such as a dream of flying like a bird; but in some metaphorical yet very real way, that dream *is* about "flying." The motif of flying most likely has a special significance in the dreamer's life at the time of the dream's occurrence, and thus, the dream is making a real statement.

Acknowledging the inner *and* outer reality of the psyche is not easy given the scientific, materialistic orientation of our times, an orientation precisely to which UFO dreams and phenomena seem to be responding. As James Hillman writes, "It is easier to bear the truth of facts than the truth of fantasies."[5] One reason for this, in addition to the factor of

---

[5]James Hillman, *Re-Visioning Psychology* (New York: Harper & Row, 1975), p. 18.

our orientation, is that to bear the truth of fantasies requires a degree of insight and discretion which bearing the truth of facts does not. This is especially so when the fantasy *appears* as a fact (as in Victor's case). However, such issues are riddled with problems of their own, and as such fall into the scope of the next chapter.

CHAPTER 7

TRICK OR TREAT?

The unconscious has a great sense of humor. One way this becomes evident is when we take ourselves too seriously— or, when we take our religious experience too seriously. Such grandiosity is a sure sign we are off-track—a sure sign to everybody but ourselves. We are unconscious of our own misuse of the unconscious. This can happen to anybody who has embarked on a process of self-discovery; we tend to become attached to our discovery in an egoistic way. Instead of letting go, we inflate ourselves with an importance that is not our own. As our self-importance is inappropriate and false, the unconscious is bound to sooner or later poke fun at it. Jung called this role or aspect of the unconscious the "trickster." He borrowed the term from Paul Radin, who discovered the trickster motif in American Indian mythology. However, like Radin, Jung explored the trickster mostly in its mythological context. It was one of Jung's mentors, Théodore Flournoy, who first profiled how the playfulness and sophisticated chicanery of the unconscious can manifest in individual experience.

I vividly recall an event that happened one hot summer day a number of years ago. I was with my brother in his backyard. We were sitting in lawn chairs, drinking iced lemonades, and somehow we got into a heated debate on the inherent problems of the various helping professions—medicine, psychology, social work, etc. At one point I introduced certain principles of unconscious behavior in application to these problems, and when my brother disagreed with my analysis, I became rather critical of him. I was irritated by his lack of understanding. I eloquently pursued my ideas, eventually bringing his way of viewing things under scrutiny. I caught him on his vulnerable points, and he gave in,

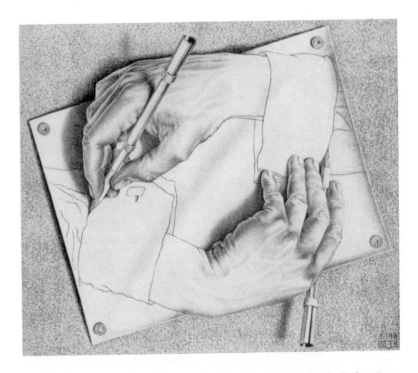

Figure 19. "The opposite of a profound truth," wrote Niels Bohr, "may well be another profound truth." Though we might think that two opposite truths could not co-exist, they in fact often even *engender* each other. The graphic artist M.C. Escher here illustrates this paradox. It is as if each truth needs to validate itself by way of contrast with its opposite. A similar principle underlies the *yin* and *yang* polarity of Taoism. M.C. Escher, *Drawing Hands*, 1948. ©1948 M. C. Escher/Cordon Art-Baarn-Holland. Used by permission.

acknowledging the value of my argument. I felt satisfied and, although I wouldn't have admitted it then, proud of myself.

After some time, I left my brother for a few moments to go out to my car to get my sunglasses because the sun was at such an angle that it was glaring into our eyes. As I was closing the door of my car after retrieving my glasses, I heard a loud screech down the block. I looked up and saw a peculiar sight for this quiet, residential neighborhood. A large black limousine—the kind movie stars ride in—had screeched around the corner and was coming down the street at a very rapid speed. Its shiny blackness in the sun was ominous, especially when I realized that the windows were so heavily tinted that I could not see into the car. The car started to weave back and forth from one side of the street to the other. It was coming towards me about forty miles per hour. I was standing at the side of my car that was facing inwards to the street. It looked like I was going to be hit! My heart started skipping beats. I wondered what maniac or drunkard could be driving this car: I couldn't see anybody. When the car was about twenty feet from me, I looked at the license plate. In bold black letters against a yellow background, it said, EGO. The car came dangerously close, missing me by perhaps four feet. I had to jump onto the hood of my car for protection.

I could not help but laugh when I calmed down and connected this incident with my previous discussion and state of mind. It seemed very appropriate. Perhaps it was all a coincidence. But then again, perhaps not.

Experiences of this kind are one matter when they happen on a small scale. They are a different matter when we are so locked into our own points of view that we altogether miss the messages the unconscious sends to us. Especially when our points of view are endowed with religious significance and have the numinosity of the *mysterium tremendum* about them, we are not likely to let them easily go. We ultimatize; we get fixed on permanent truths; we don't want to live in the unknown; we want everything to be known. Yet

Figure 20. The first of 78 cards in the tarot deck is The Fool. It is from the condition of the fool—from the folly of our not knowing, our ignorance—that wisdom originates. Of course, the tarot is referring specifically to the fool for God—one who possesses a certain kind of wisdom but is, nevertheless, not grounded in the practical reality of the everyday world. Here The Fool, in his youthful spirit of confidence and joyful aspiration, is moving toward greater heights, but if he is not careful he may fall off the mountain. In psychological terms, a fool for God is a victim of what Jung called an inflation, an overidentification of the ego with the unconscious. He is not ego-tripping as much as "unconscious-tripping"; he is so enamored with the "profundity of it all" that he can't get enough, and so the profundity—the unconscious—comes to possess him in a manic way. Card taken from the Rider Waite Tarot Deck conceived by Arthur Edward Waite, and published by U.S. Games. Used by permission.

the impossibility of this desire ever being met puts us into a paradoxical predicament. And the more we seek to solve it, the farther we get from the solution.

The "solution," if one can call it such, seems to be to accept, as the physicist Niels Bohr observed, that for every profound truth there may exist an opposite yet equally pro-found truth.[1] God did not create the Devil simply because he needed a fall guy to prove how good he is. The "Devil," or that which is opposite to God, is there almost as if to show that the universe can be single and yet still be so diverse as to be turned against itself. The unconscious takes no exception to this, and if we become obsessed with an absolute truth or belief-system about reality, the unconscious, too, may turn against us. However, this revolt against our egoistic spiritu-ality is less often in the form of a punishment than a joke. The fact that it is a joke is what makes it so punishing, or humiliating. This seems to be the purpose of the trickster: to humor, to humiliate, to humble. And yet, it is in this hum-bling that the trickster reveals his true role and intentions as the Great Teacher. Trickster episodes and phenomena are not punishments but lessons, and for this reason, as Blake writes, does the fool who persists in his folly eventually find wisdom.

It is in this light that I wish to turn our attention to trickster phenomena. I see such phenomena as byproducts of our overzealous appetites to make the unknown known— byproducts which, for many of us, are par for the course. Usually, when we recognize that these products or pseudo-truths have been manufactured by our unconscious as read-ily as the "true" truths, we pass them by, or they altogether disappear. Until that time, however, we remain in their grip.

In the following I'd like to discuss a couple of examples of what may be trickster phenomena. No criticism or judg-ment is intended, for, again, such phenomena seem to be the

---

[1] Cited in Gary Taubes, "Einstein's Dream," *Discover: The Newsmagazine of Science* (New York: Time, Inc., December 1983), p. 53.

unconscious' response to our very human—even if overzeal-ous—appetites. I would also hope that I have learned some-thing from my episode with my brother. In the spirit of that experience, I will here not try to prove any points or argu-ments, but merely suggest certain explanations for the reader to reflect upon.

ॐ

In 1975, a man described by Aldous Huxley as "one of the most brilliant minds in parapsychology"[2] underwent an extraordinary series of experiences. Being a parapsycholo-gist, Dr. Andrija Puharich is no stranger to such experiences, and one might argue that he is even predisposed to them. Puharich is the author of *The Sacred Mushroom* (1959), *Beyond Telepathy* (1962), and *Uri: A Journal of the Mystery of Uri Geller* (1974). Although it is for his work with the Israeli psychic Uri Geller that he is best known, Puharich is also acknowledged for his numerous electronic inventions. One of these includes a device which administers radio waves of specific frequencies directly to the skin, accelerating the healing process in bone fractures and controlling blood clotting. Puharich is a physician by training, and thus his background is in science.

Stuart Holroyd's book, *Briefing for the Landing on Planet Earth*, comprehensively describes Puharich's 1975 experi-ence. Puharich had joined forces with Sir John Whitmore and a medium named Phyllis Schlemmer. He discovered that Schlemmer was a medium not only for spirits from other dimensions, but extraterrestrials from other planets. Schlemmer would enter a trance state, and communications directed specifically to Puharich and Whitmore would emerge. The communications, conveyed regularly over a lengthy period of time, came from another galaxy, from a group of advanced beings known as "the Management." A

---

[2]Cited in Stuart Holroyd, *Briefing for the Landing on Planet Earth* (London: W.H. Allen, 1979), p. 9. Used by permission.

two-way dialogue ensued, and eventually the communications developed into a complex program of instructions aimed at preventing nuclear holocaust on earth, on raising the general level of consciousness in society, and on preparing the planet for a mass landing of UFOs from this other galaxy. The purpose of the landing would be to help guide the world through this difficult period of its history and to insure that it attains the goal of its evolution. This goal was characterized as a highly evolved stage of spirituality.

Offhand, one would be inclined to dismiss Puharich as a quack and his experience, or his acceptance of his experience at face value, as a form of self-deception. However, Schlemmer's trance states and the communications that arose from them cannot be dismissed by a simple wave of the hand. As Holroyd astutely observes, many of the philosophic concepts which surfaced in the communications had strong parallels with the Gnostic tradition, a syncretism of Egyptian, Babylonian, Greek, Persian, and Jewish teachings. In addition, the communications were accompanied by very impressive paranormal phenomena. The supposed beings who were believed to be responsible for the communications consistently demonstrated precognitive knowledge and clairvoyance. There were occasions of materialization and dematerialization of objects, as well as synchronicities which suggested that higher powers were arranging events. Some of these occurrences were witnessed by the respected scientist Lyall Watson, who was invited to sit in on a number of the communication sessions. If such occurrences do not automatically prove the veracity of the source of the communications, they do at least show why Puharich was so awed by them, for certainly, *something* was going on. The question is, what?

Around the turn of the century, Flournoy and Myers documented a number of fascinating cases involving mediums and knowledge derived from trance states. In one study, Flournoy described a young mother who periodically dictated lengthy excerpts from philosophical writings that were well outside the scope of her interests and education.[3] Information about deceased people's lives was also in some cases found to be uncannily factual. Yet for the most part, Flournoy and Myers found that although the communications of mediums were highly informative, much of the information given, as well as its alleged source, could be demonstrated to be factually inauthentic. They were not historically veridical. Both information and purported source seemed to be the products of the vivid imagination of the unconscious, of its penchant for weaving stories of a fantastic nature. This became especially evident when the sources were claimed to be spirit or extraterrestrial entities from such planets as Mars.

Flournoy and Myers called this story-inventing tendency of the unconscious the mythopoetic function. Jung attributed this function to the autonomous complexes, and believed that they were most often the sources responsible for medium and trance communications. In Jung's view, the trickster is an archetypal personality, a primitive form of the hero archetype, who is in turn a primitive form of the self archetype.[4] The significance of the trickster being on the lower end of the same continuum that the self is on shall shortly become evident.

The fact that the trickster is an archetypal complex explains much. Like any autonomous complex, it can act with intelligence, disseminating knowledge and ordering paranormal events into a meaningful pattern. We see these features in Puharich's experience. We also see material of a distinctly archetypal nature. The idea of a massive fleet of UFOs coming to earth with the purpose to save us and spiritually guide us is essentially a messianic idea. The messianic

---

[3]Théodore Flournoy, *Congrès International de Psychologie*, Munich, 1896, pp. 417–420. Also cited in Henri F. Ellenberger, *The Discovery of the Unconscious: The History and Evolution of Dynamic Psychiatry* (New York: Basic Books, 1970), p. 317.

[4]The hero archetype embodies our aspiration to attain heroic heights of achievement, power, and mastery. The self archetype is by contrast more oriented toward the attainment of knowledge and wisdom.

idea—that there will come a point in history at which God will reveal himself and the world will be transformed into a godly state—is a core idea of Judeo-Christianity.

There have been times when both Judaism and Christianity have been preoccupied with the Messiah's arrival, expecting it to be imminent. During the Middle Ages this expectation often reached feverish heights, giving rise to messianic or millennial movements. People lived as if the "last days" were here; they gave up their possessions and homes to follow some charismatic figure who managed to capture their imaginations and pose as the Messiah's harbinger. In Judaism, such movements arose during periods when the Jews were especially persecuted and oppressed; in Christianity, they tended to develop during times of social upheaval, crisis in religious belief, plague, and of course, toward the end of the first millennium. The hope was that the Messiah would come and bring in a new age. Many anticipate such a "New Age" now—as we approach a new millennium and are also beset with global problems—and it is not surprising that Puharich's experience is so messianic and millennial in tone.

The force of the messianic idea is not to be underestimated. Being thousands of years old, it is archetypal and ingrained into the very constitution of the psyche—at least the Western psyche. Some have called it the messianic complex, implying—as Freud did with the Oedipus complex, and Jung with all archetypal complexes—that it has its own edifice or structure within the psyche. It exercises unique dynamics of behavior and drives us with a relentless energy. The rise of such messianic movements as Nazism, the Iranian revolution, and the general cultlike glorification of Hollywood idols shows that this complex can still very much seize us. In its drive to find a savior or redeeming qualities which we feel we don't have but want, this complex can attach itself to almost any numinous figure or, as in Puharich's case, "mission."

As Bob Dylan commented, evidently reflecting on his own experience in these matters, it is not the belief in a particular Messiah that is important here, but the messianic complex, the instinctive force behind the belief.[5] Experiences like Puharich's seem to tap right into this archetypal, instinctive force. That one should become identified with it is almost inevitable. Puharich is told: "You are the proclaimer."[6] Instructed by the beings to travel to various places of international political conflict and meditate there with the intent of diffusing healing and helping energy, Puharich, Whitmore, and Schlemmer undertake a messianic mission. They alone can do it: "It is important that the power that the three of you generate negates the Soviet Russia's thinking. It is also of the utmost importance that you be in Israel not later than the twenty-fourth of your November. . . . It is through your energy that the leaders of Israel will be given the strength to make the proper decisions and proper negotiations without giving their souls."[7] Apparently in the same way that capitalism is driven by the profit motive, messianism is driven by the prophet motive.

Experiences like Puharich's can tell us much about the ways the unconscious can appeal to us. To differentiate what is genuine from what is the trickster may itself be tricky. It is almost as if the unconscious is, through such experiences, testing us to determine how "trickable" we are, how mature we are, by seeing how we deal with the demanding responsibility of evaluating what is "true" and what is not: do we actively assume this responsibility, or do we leave it to the unconscious? Or perhaps the unconscious is testing us by subtly attempting to *take* the responsibility from us upon itself. The question then is, do we let it? Faith in the unconscious without discretion and understanding is no different than blind trust and subservience, and this can have tricksterish consequences. Perhaps it was the lure of such callings from the unconscious that prompted Christ to warn that many are called but few are chosen. However, before we

---

[5]Bob Dylan, *Spin*, December 1985, p. 81.
[6]Cited in Stuart Holroyd, *op. cit.*, p. 218.
[7]Cited in Stuart Holroyd, *op. cit.*, p. 199. Used by permission.

turn to the finer task of differentiating among the unconscious' manifestations, I would like to provide one more
example of a likely trickster episode so that it should not
seem that Puharich's was an isolated instance.

の

If Puharich is not a household name, Elisabeth Kübler-
Ross most probably is. Her books, most notably *On Death
and Dying* and *Questions and Answers on Death and Dying*,[8] are
internationally acclaimed. As a physician and psychiatrist,
Kübler-Ross was one of the first to broach the topic of dying,
treating it as a natural aspect of life *and* of medical practice,
something we all need to face at some point. Her pioneering
work with terminally ill patients revealed what has now
become classically known as the five stages of facing death;
but moreover, Kübler-Ross' work has raised the awareness
of the medical establishment, enabling it to approach death
and the process of dying in a more enlightened and humane
way.

In the mid-1970s, Kübler-Ross' work with the dying took
a marked spiritual, or perhaps one should say, spiritistic
turn. She became involved with a group of mediums who
claimed to be able to materialize spirit beings; these beings
would act as spiritual guides and healers. The mediums,
particularly a man named Jay Barham, assembled a following of about two hundred people. A scandal broke out when
twenty members of this assembly reported that the material-
ized spirit-forms were really Barham and other mediums in
disguise; this apparent sleight of hand could easily occur
because the spirits could materialize only in darkness. The
members further claimed that the "spirit guides" had
engaged them in sexual activity. When it was alleged that a
10-year-old girl had been sexually molested by one of the

---

[8]Elisabeth Kübler Ross, *On Death and Dying* (New York: Macmillan, 1970)
and *Questions and Answers on Death and Dying* (New York: Macmillan,
1974).

guides, the San Diego District Attorney's Office conducted an investigation.

The scandal reached national proportions when it was learned that Kübler-Ross, although not knowing anything about the supposed sexual encounters, was actively involved with the group. She denounced the allegations and came out in full support of Barham. Her continued work with him and her insistence on the authenticity of the spirit materializations led to a deterioration of her credibility with the scientific community, as well as to the demise of her twenty-year marriage: her husband left her. Obviously, like Puharich, Kübler-Ross takes her experience very seriously. Both hear the beat of a different drummer and are prepared to follow it at all costs.

How can we understand the motivation for Kübler-Ross' unshakeable conviction? Is it simply that she wanted to believe, and in her desire and gullibility did so, as some have suggested? Or could there have been other factors influencing her judgment? In a candid *Playboy* interview, Kübler-Ross explains the circumstances which led to her discovery of spirit guides. In 1972, she participated in a series of laboratory exercises conducted by Robert Monroe, an engineer who had developed a technique for facilitating out-of-body experiences. These exercises resulted in two out-of-body experiences which Kübler-Ross claims were very rejuvenating and which healed an abdominal disease from which she was suffering. Shortly after this she had what sounds like a mystical experience of agony and ecstasy:

> . . . it hit me like lightning. . . . I had become *every* patient I ever attended, and I went through the deaths of *every* single person whose life I had ever touched. It was excruciating physical agony; I was doubled up in pain and felt there would be no release. I went through a thousand deaths, one right on top of the other, like labor pains but with no time to catch my breath between. But it wasn't just physical agony, it was also spiritual, emotional, every

aspect that a human could experience. . . . Suddenly a voice came from nowhere and everywhere, a very deep, loving but firm voice, a man's voice. Three and a half years later, when I met the guides, I recognized the voice. He said, "You shall not be given." And the agony continued. . . . [for] about three and a half hours. Then I asked for a hand to hold and the same voice came: "You shall not be given." The agony was unthinkable, indescribable. Suddenly, it stopped. Stopped. Then everything in the room started this high-speed vibration, everything I touched with my eyes turned into a million molecules vibrating. My belly was vibrating at the same speed and there was the bright incredible light that my patients [who had had near-death experiences] described moving toward. I merged into that light and all I can tell you is, it was like 10,000 orgasms. Everything became one and I merged into it. Two sentences came to me; one was, "I am acceptable," and the other was, "I am part of one." I fell into a trancelike sleep and later, when I walked down the hill, I was totally in love with the universe.[9]

Some years later, Kübler-Ross met Jay Barham and had her first "darkroom session" with a group of seventy-five people. A 7'10" black male, dressed like a Bedouin in a long white robe, suddenly appeared. In the same deep voice that Kübler-Ross had heard years before during her above-related experience, he announced to the group: "You are here to support this lady by creating positive energy and to continue to support her in the pursuit of her destiny." Kübler-Ross immediately accepted this event as an authentic materialization. Other events followed, most notably another spirit guide's materialization which Kübler-Ross feels is a typical example that proves such experiences are real:

---

[9]Excerpted from the *Playboy* Interview: Elisabeth Kübler-Ross, *Playboy* Magazine (May 1981) Vol. 28, pp. 69 ff; Copyright © 1981 by *Playboy*. All rights reserved. Reprinted with permission.

. . . my definition of verification might be thrown out by a hundred scientists. But when something happens like my trip to Georgia, where Mario appeared, only from the waist up, and massaged me and weeks later, when I saw him again, just to test the truth, I said, "What in the world happened in Georgia?" He played insulted and said, in that gruff voice, "Don't you remember? I gave you a back rub for 15 minutes." So, you see, I've had hundreds of these experiences. That's my verification.[10]

Putting for argument's sake the question of theatrical, sleight-of-hand tricks aside, I have to admit that if I saw what I thought was a being whose body appeared only from the waist up, I too would think that something extraordinary was going on. In fact, even considering the theatrical and other seriously questionable elements of Kübler-Ross' story, I am inclined to think that what Kübler-Ross experienced *was* real. As the reader can surmise from the preceding chapters, I am of the impression that the unconscious mind is capable of almost anything. However, to present the opposite truth of a proposition I raised in the first chapter—Do events have to be real in order to be true?—I would here make the following qualification: simply because an event is real does not mean it is true. Said otherwise, I believe that Kübler-Ross, like Puharich, probably experienced extraordinary paranormal occurrences. They were real. That they were encounters with genuinely higher, spiritual beings engaged in a mission to enlighten humankind is probably not literally true, but rather a fiction or fantasy of the unconscious.[11]

What is however true about such unconscious fictions—if not their presenting "facts"—is that they are powerful

---

[10]*Playboy* Interview with Elisabeth Kübler-Ross, p. 102–103. Copyright © 1981 by *Playboy*. All rights reserved. Reprinted with permission.

[11]Like Puharich's beings, Kübler-Ross' beings are here in order to diminish the negativity that exists in our world and to prevent nuclear holocaust. Again we see the "Armageddon" motif emerging, as it has for thousands of years in people's visions and mystical experiences, though granted, it is

encounters with the intrinsic spirituality of the unconscious. Perhaps what it takes for certain people to recognize this spirituality is precisely such a jarring, paranormal experience. Perhaps Kübler-Ross *needed* "spirits" and Puharich *needed* "extraterrestrials" to really "see"—although it is apparent they were already "seekers"—that there is a higher intelligence in the universe, a higher order behind what we see with our eyes. It is in connection with this principle—namely, the need to literally, physically see—that we may unearth the more hidden implications of trickster phenomena.

♨

The trickster comes when we are too attached to our religious point of view or are too eager to make the unknown known in an absolute way. If in addition to this eagerness we have very large expectations of what would be fitting for a manifestation of the unknown, we will need great revelations or epiphanies to satisfy our appetite. It was conceivably in response to this that Christ taught that those who have faith without having witnessed miracles are more blessed than those who need them. For he probably sensed the danger of our needs: our unconscious just might oblige us. Miracles, or great paranormal productions, are often allusions to truth that have a strange blend of allusion and illusion. We see this in the experiences of both Puharich and Kübler-Ross: there was much in their experiences that pointed to higher truth, e.g., Gnostic teachings, mystical consciousness, etc., but there was also, it seems, much fiction.

One way to view this mixture of truth with fiction is the way mythologists view myths or the way artists understand art. "Art," Picasso said, "is a lie which makes us realize the

---

[11](cont.) especially relevant in our modern, nuclear age. Also, as with Puharich, we see Kübler-Ross being cast into a messianic role: she is being especially groomed to diminish this negativity in the world through her newly found spiritual knowledge. And, like a Messiah, her mission is one of martyrdom: "I believe absolutely that I will have to make great sacrifices to bring what I've learned to the world." The belief in one's special and costly "election" is a common feature of unconscious fictions.

Figure 21. The works of this Russian-born artist aim to impart lies more telling than the truth. This two-panel painting (Panel B on page 195) is a reflection on the nature of propaganda, both in the political sense and in the wider, cultural sense. Anton Vidokle, *Idyllia, Panel A*, New York, 1990. Oil on canvas, 72″ × 72″. Used by permission.

Figure 22. Anton Vidokle, *Idyllia, Panel B*, New York, 1990. Oil on canvas, 8" × 8". Used by permission.

truth." However, the danger here is that one may focus on the lie or flashy, miraculous fiction to such an extent that it overshadows the truth. Instead of simply acknowledging the message—e.g., there is a higher intelligence and order of reality—and *letting it go* at that, one becomes almost hypnotized by the fiction, by the story through which the message is presented. And, as any skilled storyteller could attest, good fiction begets more fiction. With such experiences we must develop a discerning eye with which to separate the message from the medium (pardon the pun), otherwise we may indeed believe, as Marshall McLuhan would say but with different intentions of course, that "the medium is the message." What we are really saying here is that we should be careful—as the Zen adage advises—to not mistake the finger pointing to the moon for the moon. The exploration of the unconscious must always be an exercise in moderation and critical reflection. The Trickster loves to play.

Earlier we raised the idea that the trickster is on the same psychic continuum as the self; the former is on the lower end, the latter on the higher. Roberto Assagioli, the psychologist and founder of psychosynthesis, had his own conception of this continuum and came to an important conclusion about it. Curiously, Diana Becchetti, the wife of Sir John Whitmore, was a student of Assagioli's at the time Whitmore was involved with Puharich and Schlemmer. Holroyd writes about a discussion he had with Becchetti during this time:

> In a conversation with me, Diana said of Assagioli: "He believed that certain things were lower psychism and certain things were higher, in the sense that lower psychism was astral projection, telepathy, clairvoyance, mediumship, whereas higher psychism was intuition, illumination, inspiration, and he felt very much that if we tune into and focus all our attention on the lower aspects of psychism we won't allow the higher development to occur." What

worried Diana about the communications and John's involvement was that she felt that there was a good deal of lower psychism involved in them.[12]

This distinction between what is essentially a lower form of religious experience and a higher form is one I have also noticed on many occasions, both in regard to others and myself. The tone people speak in when sharing a deep illumination is very different than when sharing a psychic experience. Paranormal occurrences may be interesting and exciting, but they usually do not foster much spiritual insight into ourselves or life; in fact, they often have nothing to do with things of a divine nature, though they may appear to. For the most part, they seem to be just "happenings," albeit extraordinary happenings.

The distinguishing terms I prefer to use for lower and higher forms of religious experience are "magical" and "mystical." "Magical" would include paranormal experiences, or anything that has a certain magic about it. It could include occult magic, though the quality I wish to emphasize is the semblance of the miraculous, the extraordinary. "Mystical," however, is on a different level. As the theologian Malcolm Spicer remarked, "The mystical is not extra-ordinary. It is ordinary—*very* ordinary. The problem is that people do not experience the ordinary." The mystical is the transcendent or divine experienced in everyday life, in the commonplace; it is the experience of the divine and the commonplace as identical. Thus, if magical (and in particular trickster) experiences teach us that all that shines is not made of gold, mystical experience teaches us that all that is gold need not shine, at least not with the blinding brilliance we might anticipate. Furthermore, as an encounter with the supreme intelligence, mystical experience is a mainspring for spiritual understanding and wisdom—qualities which most magical experiences do not engender. Of course, as often happens, a mystical

---

[12]Stuart Holroyd, *Briefing for the Landing on Planet Earth*, p. 107.

Figure 23. Shakespeare's Puck, in *A Midsummer Night's Dream*, is a wonderful example of a trickster figure. He goes about casting spells upon the unsuspecting, allowing them to create a web of confusion out of their own desires and delusions. He is a mischievous imp, and although he is by no means evil or diabolical, his playfulness has sharp teeth. But he has a lesson to teach:

> *If we shadows have offended,*
> *Think but this, and all is mended,*
> *That you have but slumber'd here*
> *While these visions did appear.*
> *And this weak and idle theme,*
> *No more yielding but a dream . . . .*

Engraving from a painting by Henry Fuseli (1741–1825). Quotation from William Shakespeare, *A Midsummer Night's Dream*, Act V, Scene I, lines 430–35.

experience may also be magical, or paranormal, but it is the direct encounter with this intelligence that is most salient, and not the time-and-space fireworks.

It is true, as Assagioli indicated, that many people "get stuck" in the fireworks of the magical and never get to see the pristine light of the mystical. There are two ways to approach this spiritual problem or impasse: one is through it and the other is around it. Let us speak of the first first.

Jung's way of growth is to work through complexes. The trickster or lower end of the continuum, if that is what one is experiencing, must simply be worked through. However, just because this is a lower or primitive form of the self does not mean it is contemptible or "evil." Even if it were evil, one would have to work with it; it is an aspect of one's psyche. The point is, it *can be* worked with. The fact that the trickster and the self are on the same continuum means not only that they are related to each other; it means that the trickster is the self in disguise—in a childlike, playful form, let us say—and the self is the trickster in a mature, evolved form. This latter form emerges as one matures and grows through—or rather outgrows—the trickster to come upon a more refined and authentic appreciation of the self.

Jung offers an interesting illustration of this concept in a passage from his *Alchemical Studies*. He is here elaborating upon the work of the 16th-century physician and alchemist Paracelsus. In particular, he is commenting on typical trickster phenomena which the alchemists experienced and how they dealt with them:

> It is Adech, the inner man [the self], who with his Scaiolae [spirit forces] guides the purpose of the adept and causes him to behold fantasy images from which he will draw false conclusions, devising out of them situations of whose provisional and fragile nature he is unaware. . . .

The "acts of Melusina" [a nymphlike spirit who comes from the deep waters and practices magic] are deceptive phantasms compounded of supreme sense and the most pernicious nonsense, a veritable veil of Maya [illusion] which lures and leads every mortal astray. From these phantasms the wise man will extract the "supermonic" elements, that is, the higher aspirations; he extracts everything meaningful and valuable as in a process of distillation, and catches the precious drops of the *liquor Sophiae* [liqueur of Wisdom] in the ready beaker of his soul, where they "open a window" for his understanding. Paracelsus is here alluding to a discriminative process of critical judgment which separates the chaff from the wheat—an indispensable part of any rapprochement with the unconscious. It requires no art to become stupid; the whole art lies in extracting wisdom from stupidity. Stupidity is the mother of the wise, but cleverness never.[13]

Thus, we see not only Jung's approach, but the value he places on such phenomena if we can filter out from them what represents the self as opposed to the trickster.

The second approach is that of Buddhists and mystics in general.[14] Zen Buddhists call trickster phenomena *makyo*. These include visions, fantasies, revelations, hallucinations, and illusory sensations. In Japanese, the word *makyo* means "the devil's realm," yet this does not imply that *makyo* are inherently evil; rather, they can have disturbing or "diabolical" effects if, as Philip Kapleau writes, "one is ignorant of their true nature and is ensnared by them."[15]

---

[13]From *The Collected Works of C. G. Jung*, translated by R.F.C. Hull, Bollingen Series XX. Vol. 13, *Alchemical Studies*, pp. 179–80. Copyright © 1967 by Princeton University Press. Used by permission.

[14]Indeed, one will find, for example, that the approach St. John of the Cross takes to trickster phenomena is almost identical to that of the Buddhists.

[15]Philip Kapleau, *The Three Pillars of Zen*, p. 38.

An interesting story revealing the Zen approach to such phenomena is related by a student of the modern Zen master Koun Yamada. Yamada was the abbot or head master of the renowned Harada-Yasutani school of Zen Buddhism; he inherited this position from his predecessor Hakuun Yasutani. Sometime after Yasutani died, this student was practicing meditation in the meditation hall with the other students. She was sitting on her meditation cushion, intensely engaged. Suddenly, she saw a vivid apparition of Yasutani standing beside the altar, watching everybody with a smile of satisfaction on his face. Distracted, she could no longer focus on her meditation. The apparition, apparently visible only to her, persisted. Having requested a private interview with Zen Master Yamada, she told him what she saw. "Very interesting," said the Zen master. "It may be real, and it may not. But that is not your purpose here. You are here to discover your true nature. Now go back to your cushion and resume your practice."

The student went back to her cushion and resumed her practice. The apparition disappeared.

EPILOGUE

It is a generally accepted fact that the appeal of traditional religion has declined. Though there are still many who follow traditional faiths wholeheartedly and without reservation, more and more of us are questioning the existence of God and whether the soul is really something with ultimate and eternal significance. Compared to former times, when religious values were rarely questioned and were intrinsic to everyday life, we are today in a spiritual eclipse. What was obvious to the ancients and medievals is in darkness for us. It is no accident that Pope John Paul II, in his world travels, finds the greatest number of new converts to Christianity in the Third World, especially Africa; for here the openness to the idea of God acting as a real force in the world of time and space has not yet altogether succumbed to the ways of modernity.

A variety of reasons may be cited as to why this eclipse in spiritual belief and values is occurring. Historians and philosophers attribute it to the rise of the scientific, secular worldview late in the last century. This led to a disenchantment with our religious "mythology" (namely, the Bible), which no longer could be accepted as literal truth. The impact of this emerging worldview was prophetically proclaimed by Nietzsche when he screamed, "God is dead!," meaning in particular the Judeo-Christian *idea* of God. Evidently, he had foreseen that scientific materialism would make it appear obsolete.

Our ability to annihilate ourselves with nuclear weapons and our leap into outer space have further made traditional ideas of deity and the scheme of things seem anachronistic, for now our place in the universe can no longer be seen as assured or as significant as it once was. However, regardless of the complex fabric of reasons underlying this large-scale, civilizational change, the fact remains: the world, the cosmos, no longer reveals a higher order, a supreme intelligence; it is just nature – to be conquered and manipulated for technological, material gain. We no longer perceive a divine presence in it or in our lives. God has disappeared from our horizons.

Of course, there have been a number of reactions to this state of affairs, such as the theosophical and, more recently, New Age movements. Certain schools of psychology – particularly Jung and existentialists like Frankl, Maslow, and May – represent such reactions as well. All reflect attempts to keep the flame of the soul kindled in the night of our spiritual eclipse. But the task is difficult: the less we see God, the more we want tangible proof that he exists. And reversely, the more we want tangible proof, the less we see. It is a different, more experiential kind of proof and "seeing" that is needed.

It is in light of this that I have written this book. My aim has been to show that the unconscious is a window to the soul and to God, to the magic and mystery that is within each of us. At a time when religious truths no longer appear certain and faith is dubious, the unconscious remains a "sure thing," always present and accessible. However, there exist strong differences of opinion as to what the unconscious in fact is, what is its essential nature. Psychology is less than a hundred-and-fifty years old and is steeped in the same scientific materialism that defines the subject matter and methodology of the other natural sciences. (Although psychology has evolved into a social and human science, it had its beginnings in physiology.) Freud's views on the mind, for instance, were distinctly colored by scientific materialism insofar as he saw the mind as a system of libidinal energy – instinctual impulses – that, to a large extent, operates according to hydraulic principles. He conceived the unconscious, or id, as a reservoir of libido that is controlled by the ego and superego the same way the locks of a dam regulate its water supply.

A similar kind of mechanistic thinking permeates the study of psychology in America and American universities – as observable in behavioral psychology, for example – and it is for this reason that the less empirical and more mystical Jung is so frowned upon here. Yet even Jung, upon whom I have relied so preponderantly in this book, would have been hard put with the degree to which I have advocated the unconscious' essential identity as God. Clearly, although this is a book about the unconscious, it is not one with which the more "psychologically" minded reader might agree. However, such readers are reminded that the unconscious was not discovered by modern psychology. The Romantics knew and wrote about it, almost all mystical traditions speak of it in one form or another, and Vedanta and Tibetan Buddhism in particular have complex systems of epistemology that elaborate various of its subtler processes. All these traditions believe that the unconscious is supraordinate to the conscious mind (as opposed to psychology which holds that the unconscious is a subcategory of the mind); that this unconscious is related to a purposive and intelligent Nature (as opposed to the evolving but blind, nonteleological nature of scientific materialism); and that Nature is in turn the instrument of God, if not God himself. Of course, one could argue that this claim of an intrinsic unity between the unconscious and God is purely an Old World view. This may be so, but simply because it is old or prescientific does not mean it is antiquated or without validity. Ageless ideas always find a way of resurfacing and of compelling us to pay them their due.

What does it mean to say that the unconscious mind and God are essentially one? It is to say that God has assumed a place within our souls, the place where he is "soul-making," to borrow a term from Blake and Keats. If we can see his soul-making—the sundry, dreamlike things he does in and through our psyches—we may catch a glimpse of him, and who knows? perhaps more than a glimpse. Yet sometimes I wonder if the unconscious is really a natural habitat for God, if it is truly his preferred sanctuary. Perhaps he has been imprisoned there by us precisely because we have pushed him out of our everyday, conscious awareness. The more we have pushed him out, the deeper he has retreated into the unconscious.

This possibility of God's retreat into the unconscious also appears to have been anticipated in Old World views. According to many religions, there was a time—albeit a metaphorical time—when God was always close-at-hand and foremost in our awareness. We have devolved, not evolved. This notion is captured not only in the myth of Atlantis, the lost civilization in which the mind was supposedly developed beyond current levels. It is also conveyed in the myth of the Garden of Eden. There, Adam and Eve traveled freely in a paradisaic state of mind; they were created "in the image of God." They knew God directly. But when the fruit from the tree of the knowledge of good and evil—the dualistic, egoistic mind—took hold, humankind was banished from the Garden, seeking to return ever since. Our original condition was lost (resulting in the so-called original sin). With Christ, however, the myth of exile reached a new juncture: "the kingdom of heaven is within you." The original condition still exists. Christ was perhaps here alluding to something like the unconscious mind. Turning within, one finds God, and by finding him, releases him from *his* exile.[1]

---

[1]Certain theories on the origins of consciousness, such as those of Erich Neumann and Julian Jaynes, may be seen as providing a psychological parallel to the mythic idea of exile. These theories suggest that at an earlier

Of course, I would not want to seriously portray the unconscious in terms of a prison, not even as the prison of God. For as we have seen, the unconscious is a magnificent and bountiful phenomenon, one perhaps especially suited to be a choice sanctuary for God. In this book we have heard the testimonies of artists, writers, scientists, statesmen, athletes, and others. We have seen how the unconscious has contributed to their creative efforts, warned them of impending danger by exercising its paranormal abilities, and enriched their understanding of life by imbuing them with mystical insights. We have seen how the unconscious is not just within us, but all around us, unifying us with the spatio-temporal realm and revealing it to be a fluid state within the mind of the cosmos, God's mind. In this state, magic can become real, for God, too, likes to dream and to play. And in his dream-plays, our delusions may also assume a reality. UFOs may appear or may communicate to us "supreme sense and the most pernicious nonsense," and spirit guides may appear to us half-materialized and delight us with back massages. Indeed, the unconscious seems to be an appropriate abode for a mysterious God whose thoughts are not the thoughts of men.

---

[1](cont.) stage of evolution the unconscious was more directly accessible to us, but with the emergence of a dominating ego-consciousness, the unconscious became dissociated; as a result we lost our direct and frequent contact with it and with the world of God through it. However, in supporting mythic ideas with modern parallels, we must not overlook the hidden "meta-messages" which are part and parcel of any myth. If in the Garden of Eden there existed a tree whose fruits could cause our exile, we must ask, "Who planted this tree, and why?" One answer is that our exile marks the beginning of our freedom—yes, freedom even from God—to find God on our own initiative. The world of ego-consciousness—of the knowledge of good and evil—has it own value (as modern theorists would also contend), and to discover, after having been in this world, a paradise once lost is to appreciate it in a new and unique way. Apparently, God did not intend for us to take him or our own Godhood for granted.

The still good hand of God reaches out to us from this abode. It may spark in us a sense of joy and awe, or a feeling of relatedness to the love and intelligence behind it. Or, in times of struggle or grief, it may infuse a touch of its stillness into our lives, reminding us that beneath the turbulent waves—and yes, even within them—everything is all right. God is still here.

The hand of God may emerge through a wide variety of circumstances, and always unexpectedly. We cannot force it; it comes as an act of grace, almost as an accident. As one Zen master put it, the most our religious efforts can do is make us accident-prone. We can only prepare for God's hand— should it indeed reach out to us—and strive to meet it half-way with our own open, helping hand. Though our effort demands our passion and persistence to sustain it, it has but a simple requirement. All we have to do, finally, is keep a prayerful attitude and an attentive gaze inward—inward into ourselves, and inward into the heart of the world.

THE DREAM JOURNAL

The dream journal consists of a series of exercises. The first involves a kind of meditation or directed concentration that will help you to remember dreams and "offer up" to the unconscious the problems you wish it to shed light upon. It is very simple. Before you go to sleep, you sit or lie on your bed and for five minutes intently tell yourself, "I will remember my dreams." You may close your eyes if you wish. If you want to wake up immediately after a dream and catch it while it is fresh in your mind, you may add, "I will wake up after important dreams." Surely, it is easier to remember a dream immediately after its occurrence, yet it is believed that the more dramatic dreams people have take place in the morning during the last cycles of REM (rapid eye movement). Thus, with practice you should be able to recall your morning dreams when you naturally awaken, and so this latter stipulation to wake up after a dream is optional. Nevertheless, it is effective and not without value for the person whose dream recollections are hazy. It works as a sort of psychological alarm clock that is set to automatically go off after a dream is completed.

After five minutes of repeating and concentrating upon the above phrases, another five-minute exercise of concentration is directed toward a particular problem or issue you wish to gain insight into. During this period of concentration, you could review the point or dilemma you are stuck on. Or, you could review the entire endeavor you are engaged in that is presenting the problem. In either case, you should not be straining yourself here or attempting to solve the problem now—otherwise you may not fall asleep. You should "carry the problem lightly" and merely form a synopsis of it in your mind, perhaps imagining it being sent into the unconscious the way a capsule or satellite is launched into space. Then you should forget about it and go to sleep. (My own personal experience with this exercise is that it often has a delayed response. That is to say, a dream response to a particular evening's meditation may not come till a few mornings later, and sometimes, many mornings later. It seems to come when I'm not anticipating it. Apparently, the unconscious either reaches or chooses to share its conclusions in its own good time.)

When you awaken in the morning, you should, if at all possible, not rush immediately out of bed. Another five-minute meditation, this one an interior "search" for the night's dreams, may help pull those dreams into consciousness. Without this effort, they tend to recede back into the night, so to speak, into the unconscious. As a dream crystallizes in consciousness, you could review it a couple of times so as to sharpen its details.

Now comes the actual recording of the dream in the journal. Preferably, this should be done immediately after a dream is remembered, though if you awaken in the middle of the night, the use of a dim night light beside your bed should allow you to briefly sketch the dream without getting out of bed. You may then readily fall back asleep and rewrite the dream more fully the next day.

The journal should be a notebook large enough to contain a lengthy period of entries. Each dream should be entered separately, and each entry should have four parts:

1. *Date* (month/day/year)

2. *Sketch* (in pencil): should you awaken in the middle of the night immediately after a dream, this is a brief, note-form sketch or "trigger" to remind you of the dream the following day when you have time to write it out in detail.

3. *Dream* (in pen): This section is a full recapitulation and description of the dream exactly how it happened and how you felt *in the dream*. It should not include conscious associations, but "just the facts." If you forget certain parts and you know this, you may indicate this so that you know where something is missing.

4. *Amplification*: This section is for exploring what the dream means. For this purpose I would recommend the Gestalt "identification technique." The reasons for this are explained below together with the technique. Of course, any conscious associations, feelings, and thoughts that come to you apart from using this technique may also be added here. The importance of this section rests on the fact that the insights unearthed here are what you potentially integrate from the dream into your everyday life.

Once a month, a *General Review* of all the month's dreams may be undertaken, with a notation of the following:

a) recurring people and animals;
b) recurring places and situations;
c) recurring events and "dramas";
d) recurring emotions, moods, and thoughts that occurred *in* the dreams;
e) significant meanings or insights that emerged in the amplification of the dreams; and
f) changes in your actual life in response to specific dreams.

Then, every three or four months (i.e., at the end of each season), these items may be compared from each month's *General Review* to see if any major patterns or messages emerge. At the end of the year, a similar review may be made.[1]

⚘

Let us turn to the amplification of a dream. The term "amplification"—first used in connection with dreams by Jung—connotes the process of expanding a dream by exploring its various shades of meaning and applications to one's life. To Frederick Perls, the founder of Gestalt therapy, this process is seen in contrast to the "interpretation" of a dream according to fixed, preconceived schemas. Having a set of ideas for what a dream symbol may mean—regardless of how profound these ideas may be—tends to limit our inquiry. Dreaming of a snake, for example, may mean a very different thing for you than it does for me, and it may mean a very different thing for you at one time compared to another time. Above all, the meaning you extract from a dream must intuitively *feel* right; it must "resonate" within you. An abstract meaning or interpretation is no more helpful than an abstract symbol.

The identification technique developed by Perls is one of the more intuitive, feeling-oriented ways of working with dreams. Perls describes it as:

> . . . quite different from what the psychoanalysts do. What's usually done with a dream is to cut it to pieces, and follow up by association what it means, and interpret it. Now we might possibly get some integration by this procedure, but I don't quite

---

[1]One person I know who kept a dream journal found in an annual review that he had dreamed a number of scenarios which he later experienced in actual life as déjà vus; he did not recognize at the time of the déjà vu episodes that they had indeed been "already seen."

believe it, because in most cases this is merely an intellectual game. . . .

In Gestalt Therapy we don't interpret dreams. We do something much more interesting with them. Instead of analyzing and further cutting up the dream, we want to bring it back to life. And the way to bring it back to life is to re-live the dream as if it were happening now. Instead of telling the dream as if it were a story in the past, act it out in the present, so that it becomes a part of yourself, so that you are really involved.[2]

Perls believes that each and every symbol in a dream—be it a person, an animal, a car, a place—represents a dissociated part of the personality, an aspect of ourselves which we are out of touch with or do not like and have hence repressed. "Since our aim is to make every one of us a wholesome person, which means a unified person, without conflicts, what we have to do is put the different fragments of the dream together. We have to *re-own* these projected, fragmented parts of our personality, and *re-own* the hidden potential that appears in the dream."[3] This is done by actively imagining ourselves to be each and every symbol, by *identifying* with each symbol in a way that animates it so that it "speaks" to us:

. . . I suggest you write the dream down and make a list of *all* the details in the dream. Get every person, every thing, every mood, and then work on these to *become* each one of them. Ham it up, and really transform yourself into each of the different items. Really *become* that thing—whatever it is in a dream—*become*

[2]From Frederick S. Perls, *Gestalt Therapy Verbatim*, p. 73. Reprinted by permission of *The Gestalt Journal*, Box 990, Highland NY 12528.
[3]*Ibid.*, pp. 71–72.

it. Use your magic. Turn into that ugly frog or whatever is there—the dead thing, the live thing, the
demon—and stop thinking. Lose your mind and
come to your senses. Every little bit is a piece of the
jigsaw puzzle, which together will make up a much
larger whole—a much stronger, happier, more completely *real* personality.

Next, take each one of these different items, characters, and parts, and let them have encounters
between them. Write a script. By "write a script," I
mean have a dialogue between the two opposing
parts and you will find—especially if you get the correct opposites—that they always start out fighting
each other. All the different parts—any part in the
dream is yourself, is a projection of yourself, and if
there are inconsistent sides, contradictory sides, and
you use them to fight each other, you have the eternal conflict game, the self-torture game. As the process of encounter goes on, there is a mutual learning
until we come to an understanding, and an appreciation of differences, until we come to a oneness and
integration of the two opposing forces. Then the civil
war is finished, and your energies are ready for your
struggles with the world.[4]

The list-making and scriptwriting are integral parts of
the amplification exercise in the dream journal. In becoming
a symbol, you could ask it how it feels, why it is there, what
it wants, what is its view on things, and so on. Since our
"dream egos" are actively present in most of our dreams,
and since they are bound to be involved in many of the
dialogue encounters we arrange, we may learn new things
about ourselves. It can be very enlightening—even if

---

[4]From Frederick S. Perls, *Gestalt Therapy Verbatim*, p. 74. Reprinted by
permission of *The Gestalt Journal*, Box 990, Highland, NY 12528.

painful—to hear the other people in a dream say things about us which we've never heard before or openly acknowledged. This fleshing out and interrelating of the fragmented perspectives of a dream may give rise to a view or an "existential message" (as Perls calls it) that is a genuine Gestalt. A Gestalt in this instance would be a holistic perspective that is not only the sum of its part-perspectives, but something new, something added. As a message, it is rarely if ever a statement of "what should be," but of "what is" or "what could be," i.e., what we are unconscious of; it is not moralistic but educative. It points to our hidden potential, and indeed, it is this which helps us in our struggles with the world.

SUGGESTED READING

1. *ON THE UNCONSCIOUS*
Henri F. Ellenberger, *The Discovery of the Unconscious: The History and Evolution of Dynamic Psychiatry*, Basic Books, New York, 1970.

Lyall Watson, *Lifetide: The Biology of the Unconscious*, Simon and Schuster, New York, 1979.

C.G. Jung, *Memories, Dreams, Reflections*, Vintage Books, Random House, New York, 1965.

C.G. Jung, M.-L. von Franz, Joseph L. Henderson, Jolande Jacobi, and Aniela Jaffé, *Man and His Symbols*, Dell Publishing Co., New York, 1975.

James Hillman, *Re-Visioning Psychology*, Harper and Row, New York, 1975.

Eugen Herrigel, *Zen in the Art of Archery*, Vintage Books, Random House, New York, 1971.

Hubert Benoit, *The Supreme Doctrine: Psychological Studies in Zen Thought*, Viking Press, New York, 1959.

Alan Watts, *Psychotherapy East and West*, Vintage Books, Random House, New York, 1961.

2. *ON DREAMS AND WORKING WITH DREAMS*
Louis M. Savary, Patricia H. Berne, and Strephon Kaplan Williams, *Dreams and Spiritual Growth: A Judeo-Christian Way of Dreamwork*, Paulist Press, New York/ Ramsey, New Jersey, 1984.

Ann Faraday, *Dream Power*, Berkley Publishing Group, New York, 1986.

Frederick S. Perls, *Gestalt Therapy Verbatim*, Bantam Books, New York, 1971.

Robert Bosnak, *A Little Course in Dreams*, Shambhala Publications, Boston, 1988.

Patricia Garfield, *Creative Dreaming*, Ballantine Books, New York, 1974.

Stanley Krippner (ed.), *Dreamtime and Dreamwork: Decoding the Language of the Night*, Jeremy P. Tarcher, Los Angeles, 1990.

3. *ON MEDITATION*

Lawrence LeShan, *How to Meditate: A Guide to Self-Discovery*, Bantam Books, New York, 1975.

Christmas Humphreys, *Concentration and Meditation*, Penguin Books, Baltimore, 1970.

John White (ed.), *What Is Meditation?*, Doubleday, New York, 1974.

Philip Kapleau, *The Three Pillars of Zen: Teaching, Practice, and Enlightenment*, Doubleday, New York, 1989.

Shunryu Suzuki, *Zen Mind, Beginner's Mind*, Weatherhill, New York, 1979.

Ram Dass, *Journey of Awakening: A Meditator's Guidebook*, Bantam Books, New York, 1990.

4. *ON CONTEMPLATIVE PRAYER*

Thomas Merton, *New Seeds of Contemplation*, New Directions Books, New York, 1972.

Jean-Pierre de Caussade, *Abandonment to Divine Providence*, Doubleday, New York, 1975.

Brother Lawrence of the Resurrection, *The Practice of the Presence of God*, translated by Sister Mary David, Paulist Press, New York/Ramsey, New Jersey, 1978.

Anonymous, *The Cloud of Unknowing and Other Works*, translated by Clifton Wolters, Penguin Books, New York, 1978.

Meister Eckhart, *Meister Eckhart: A Modern Translation*, translated by Raymond B. Blakney, Harper and Row, New York, 1941.

Anonymous (Joseph S. Benner), *The Impersonal Life*, Devorss & Co., Marina del Rey, California, 1941.

5. *SOME OTHER INTERESTING BOOKS WITH RELIGIOUS OR PSYCHOLOGICAL THEMES*

M. Scott Peck, *The Road Less Traveled: A New Psychology of Love, Traditional Values and Spiritual Growth*, Simon and Schuster, New York, 1978.

Robert M. Pirsig, *Zen and the Art of Motorcycle Maintenance: An Inquiry into Values*, Bantam Books, New York, 1984.

The I Ching or Book of Changes, The Richard Wilhelm Translation, Princeton University Press, Princeton, New Jersey, 1977.

Viktor E. Frankl, *Man's Search for Meaning*, Simon and Schuster, New York, 1984.

Harold Kushner, *When All You've Ever Wanted Isn't Enough*, Simon and Schuster, New York, 1987.

Carl A. Raschke, James A. Kirk, and Mark C. Taylor, *Religion and the Human Image*, Prentice-Hall, Englewood Cliffs, New Jersey, 1977.

Raymond A. Moody, Jr., *Life After Life: The Investigation of a Phenomenon—Survival of Bodily Death*, Bantam Books, New York, 1976.

Erich Fromm, *Psychoanalysis and Religion*, Yale University Press, New Haven, 1950.

Hermann Hesse, *Siddhartha*, Bantam Books, New York, 1971.

Sophy Burnham, *A Book of Angels*, Ballantine Books, New York, 1990.

Photo by Chuck Ketchel.

Michael Gellert has master's degrees in religious studies and social work. He has studied with Marshall McLuhan at the University of Toronto, and undertook Zen training with the Zen master Koun Yamada in Japan. He has worked and traveled extensively in Asia. Mr. Gellert has taught psychology and religion at Vanier College (Montreal), Hunter College of the City University of New York, and the College of New Rochelle. He was Coordinator of District Council 37's Personal Service Unit Outreach Program, an employee assistance program for the City of New York. He is currently a psychotherapist in private practice in Los Angeles, and is studying at the C.G. Jung Institute.